More Tales of Old Barnwood

Richard Auckland and Brian McBurnie

With best wishes from

Brian & Richard

Printed by
Severnprint Limited
Ashville Trading Estate
Bristol Road
Gloucester
GL2 5EU
www.severnprint.co.uk

Published by
Courtyard Books
Tarling's Yard
Church Road
Bishop's Cleeve
Cheltenham
GL52 8RN
www.courtyardbooks.co.uk
ISBN 978-0-9569436-6-8

Contents

The picture on the front cover (GRO ref. RX 35.2GS) is reproduced with the permission of Gloucestershire Archives. Several pictures of Barnwood House Hospital appear with the permission of Gloucestershire Archives and Barnwood House Trust; these are on pages 37, 38, 40, 44, 57, 58 (top), 61 (top), 67, 68, 70, 73 and the back cover (all GRO ref. D3725).

The pictures on pages 79, 87, 96 and 112 are reproduced with the permission of *The Citizen*.

The logo on page 103 is reproduced with the permission of both Earl & Thompson Marketing Limited, Gloucester and of Francis Roberts Architects, Preston. The drawing on page 105 is reproduced with the permission of Francis Roberts Architects, Preston.

Introduction

Two years ago we published "Tales of Old Barnwood". Having appreciated both the complimentary comments that were made and the fact that some people asked for more, we decided that we had just about sufficient material to warrant another book.

Again, the book is really a collection of short articles, a few of which have appeared in other publications. It includes stories and anecdotes about some of the people who have been associated with the parish. It also contains several articles about Barnwood House Hospital. The Hospital was the subject which created most interest when we gave a series of illustrated talks and so, over 40 years after it closed, we thought that this was a good opportunity to record the memories of some of its staff. A significant section of the book, therefore, is devoted to Barnwood House.

Numerous sources have been used and we have tried to make sure that we have not infringed anyone's copyright. If we have, then we sincerely apologise and ask you to contact us. We are grateful to those who have been so generous in supplying their photographs for us to use.

We would particularly like to thank Mick Ashby, Marie Baldwin, Barnwood Church, Barnwood House Trust, Barnwood School, *The Citizen*, Arthur Clive, Fay Fisher, Gloucestershire Archives, Dorothy Fry, Keith Hardwidge, Gordon Hawkes, Kay Holdaway, Lesley Iwasek, Gordon John, William Kennedy, Brian Lewis, Ken Maidstone, Middle Temple, Sheila Morgan, Trevor Morley, Robin Morris, Bob Moss, Frances Mulvey, The National Portrait Gallery, Gill Pearce, David Pobjoy, Martin Riley, Mary Seacome, John Williams and Yale Law School for their help.

Richard Auckland
Brian McBurnie
(April, 2013)

Sir Edmund Saunders

The Saunders Coat of Arms in a window
of the hall at Middle Temple.

It is not widely known that Barnwood had its very own Dick Whittington. Although many realise that Sir Edmund Saunders came from these parts and that he became a Lord Chief Justice, few are aware of the detail.

Edmund was certainly born in the parish and tradition has it that he was baptised in the font (still in use) in Barnwood Church. His baptism took place around 1630, although the records have been lost. (Incidentally, there is an argument to suggest that, although born in Barnwood, he was baptised at St Mary-de-Lode.) He lived in a cottage with his mother and stepfather somewhere at the western end of the parish. Coming from a very poor background he lacked any real education and became a beggar boy. It seems likely that he was encouraged by one of the London bound travellers, passing through the parish, to seek his fortune on the gold-paved streets of the capital. And so began a remarkable transformation.

Edmund was a very bright young man. Whilst living near Clement's Inn he persuaded the lawyers there not only to give him food but, also, to teach him to read and write. He was a quick learner; before long he was earning money as a well-regarded clerk.

His next ambition was to become a lawyer himself and he entered Middle Temple in 1660. Progress was rapid. Although the usual period of study was seven years, the benchers decided to call Edmund to the bar after only four years. In 1666 he began writing *The Reports of the Most Learned Edmund Saunders,* which was first published in 1686, with part of the detail in Latin but with the legal argument in French. These reports were, and apparently still are, highly regarded legal writings.

Saunders built up a legal practice. He defended in many important cases and he was also one of the Crown's top lawyers. He prosecuted the Earl of Shaftesbury on a charge of high treason and took on several other cases on behalf of the King. There are inferences that some of his judgements at this time may not have been entirely disinterested. Whatever, he was appointed as King's Counsel in 1682. He was knighted in January 1683 and then, soon afterwards, he was sworn in as Lord Chief Justice of the King's Bench. Sadly, his health rapidly deteriorated and he died in June of that year.

Edmund Saunders was generally regarded to be an honest man. He was keen on plants and, being very fastidious about his garden, he attached a lead label to every single plant. Having taught himself on an old virginal, he was able to play jigs upon the harpsichord. A very able lawyer, he possessed a quick wit and a sharp turn of phrase. He had little regard for fees although he became very wealthy. He was very popular with law students as they found him to be a good teacher. Saunders also had a reputation for being fond of alcohol. During one case, which concerned whether or not a certain brandy was to be subject to duty, the judge called for the jury to be shown more of the evidence. The lawyer involved had to explain that "Mr Saunders has drunk it all, My Lord".

Saunders, it seems, was not a physically attractive man. The contemporary legal biographer Roger North described him as "very corpulent and beastly; a mere lump of morbid flesh". The biographer also mentioned that Saunders was smelly and that it was rather unpleasant to be standing next to him! When describing Saunders's drinking habits, North wrote that "he was seldom without a pot of ale at his nose, or near him. That exercise was all he used; the rest of his life was sitting at his desk or piping at home; and that home was a tailor's house in Builder-Row called his lodging, and the man's wife was his nurse or worse".

When he died, Saunders left money to various charities and to several of the defendants he had assisted. He also left twenty pounds to the poor of the parish of Barnwood the place where, according to his will, "I drew my first breath".

There is no known picture of Sir Edmund and, in the opinion of the archivist at Middle Temple, it may be that given his own description of himself in his will as "so vile and loathsome as not to be endured above ground" he chose not to sit for his portrait. There are, however, a few memories. His arms appear in the heraldic glass of Middle Temple Hall and there are some gifts he made to Middle Temple. The most important donation was a Charles II silver-gilt standing cup which weighs 70 ounces and stands 14 inches high. It is inscribed with the donor's name and arms. Saunders is described in the accompanying text as "of humble origin but a master of all the technicalities of the Common Law". To date, sadly, he remains unacknowledged in his native parish.

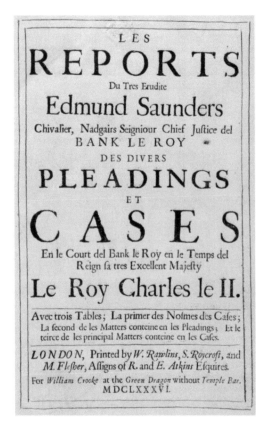

The title page from the 1686 first edition of *The Reports of the Most Learned Edmund Saunders.*

This is reproduced with the kind permission of the Rare Book Collection, Lillian Goldman Law Library, Yale Law School.

Saunders was considered to be the most accurate and valuable reporter of his age. His work was later translated into English and was still being published in the middle of the nineteenth century.

(We would like to recognise the help we received from John Williams in researching this article. We would also like to thank Lesley Whitelaw, the archivist at Middle Temple, for her assistance and for granting us permission to use the photograph of the Saunders Coat of Arms.)

The Church Chimney

There are very few old pictures of the church viewed from the south east; this one was drawn in 1874 and is signed JPM. The church chimney is clearly visible above the buttress next to the south door. During the early Holy Communion service on 4th March, 1917, there were several alarming explosions in the stove which was positioned just inside the door. These explosions, "possibly caused by the accumulation of gas from the anthracite coal", blew off part of the chimney and damaged the roof. The Alliance Fire Insurance Company made a grant of £11 towards the cost of repairing the damage. The chimney was finally removed in the middle of the 20th century.

Death and Disease

At the end of the nineteenth century, the residents of Barnwood seemed to have to cope with more than the usual degree of anxiety and misfortune. Infant deaths were sadly, as in most places, relatively common occurrences; but the sudden demise of those who were apparently fit and able members of the local community was more unusual.

An entry in the school log book, dated 8th October 1894, states that "A very sad event happened this morning. A boy in IV standard - Charles Smith, fell down in the playground in a fainting fit. I was called to him and carried him into school and did what I could to restore him sending in the meantime for his mother and the Vicar and a doctor but he died in a few minutes after being brought into the school, from failure of the heart's action. There was a half day holiday given in the afternoon".

Barely two years later, the parish magazine recorded "with great regret the death of Ernest John Berry who died early on Friday morning after a fall from a horse the previous day". Ernest had left school two years earlier to become a gardener, but he "continued to attend Sunday School until his death".

It was a huge shock to the parish when, in 1897 after only 14 months in post, Samuel Higginson "the much respected and valued Headmaster of this school" was killed at Churchdown by a Great Western Railway Company train "to the inexpressible grief of all".

The new century brought no change of fortune. In 1901, A B Evans, the Headmaster at the time, noted that "Edgar Walker was buried this afternoon. His fellow scholars and staff have subscribed to a wreath. It was placed upon the grave with the message 'Deepest sympathy. Poor little boy. Terrible sudden illness – a brief struggle, death a cold grave – and then the Great Beyond'". Edgar was 7 years old. Bernard Lodge, aged 9, died the following week.

(Incidentally, twenty years later the son of A B Evans also died in tragic circumstances as a result of wounds received in the Great War; he is remembered on the Parish War Memorial.)

Children of the time at Barnwood School.

The constant threat of illness, too, was a regular concern. Measles, diphtheria and scarlet fever affected attendance rates at the school. But the real threat was from smallpox. In 1896 Gloucester was at the centre of an epidemic which eventually claimed 443 lives in the district.

Coincidentally, this outbreak occurred exactly one hundred years after Edward Jenner performed his first experimental vaccination against smallpox. (Interestingly, a direct descendant of Jenner, Edward Jenner Noott, became Vicar of Barnwood in the 1930s.)

At this time there was some discussion about whether or not vaccination was the correct course of action. The vicar, Francis Harvie Fowler, became involved in this debate and was not afraid to air his views in the parish magazine. In February 1896 he wrote: "There is little doubt that the spread of the disease has been due to the anti-vaccination craze which has gained for our city a doubtful notoriety and not to unsanitary conditions".

Fowler went on to point out that two cases had already appeared in our area and that the Medical Officer had stated in *The Citizen* that vaccination invariably mitigates, even if it does not always prevent, an attack of smallpox.

He continued "It is sheer folly to allow the self-advertisings, the partial advocacy and cooked statistics of a few misguided faddists to weigh in the scale against the overwhelming testimony of the vast majority of scientific and medical men". Fowler added that it was everyone's duty to be vaccinated, not only to protect themselves but also to avoid being a source of danger "to the more sensible portion of the community who have been vaccinated". He finished by writing "there can be no possible objection, provided that the subjects are in good health and that only the purest calf-lymph is employed". All were entreated to take advantage of Barnwood's free vaccination programme.

> Dr. Washbourn will attend at the Barnwood Schools on Saturday, March 28th, and on every Saturday morning at 11 o'clock, until further notice, to vaccinate all persons free of charge, and with calf lymph. In view of the serious danger from delay, parents are earnestly invited to do their duty, and bring their children to be vaccinated at once, and to be re-vaccinated themselves.
> N.B.—Unvaccinated persons are a source of danger to their neighbours and to the village.

The notice, that appeared around the parish, encouraging vaccination.

Two months later, in April, Fowler deplored the fact that only 20 of the 170 pupils at the school had been vaccinated. Whilst acknowledging that, so far, there had only been a single death at the school, he intimated that there had been over 500 cases in the wider area and that one in every five had proved fatal. As the outbreak was now spreading from the city and into the county, he regarded it as "simply astounding that parents can have so little regard for the safety of their own children as to allow their obstinacy and ignorance to outweigh the testimony of science". He added that at Hucclecote "we hear that people are crowding to be vaccinated".

Four weeks later the Parish Council, which had only been formed 16 months earlier, regarded the issue as serious enough to take a "Vaccination Census". They concluded that of the 865 population in the civil parish only 207 remained at risk.

By May the tone had changed slightly. Fowler recognised that most of the children had now been vaccinated – but not the parents! Dr Washbourne had vaccinated 330 people in the free scheme and there had been some private vaccinations "but that leaves many unaccounted for". Then came the threat! Barnwood loved its annual flower show which it shared with Hucclecote. "We hope" wrote Fowler "that many who have been deaf to other arguments will listen to reason when they realise that the holding of the Flower Show now depends largely on themselves. Parishioners should understand that, if no show is held, the blame will lie at the doors of those foolish enough to decline vaccination".

Francis Harvie Fowler did not lose many arguments but, at a general meeting held on 15th May, it was unanimously resolved that "the Barnwood and Hucclecote Flower Show be not held this year". Several months later, writing his annual parish report, Fowler recalled "how mercifully we were spared during the late awful visitation of smallpox".

Joseph the Carpenter

The earliest male citizen of Barnwood of whom we have a portrait is Joseph Cullis. The Cullis family had been in the area for some years before the birth of Joseph in 1777. His baptism as "Joseph son of Michael Cullis and Sarah his wife" is recorded in the Barnwood Church Register as having taken place on November 30th of that year.

In 1801, Joseph married Jane Pockett. They had five children. One of Joseph's grandsons eventually lived in Barnwood Court and another married the sister of one of the explorers in Scott's ill-fated Antarctic expedition. Joseph's great-granddaughter, Winifred, became the first woman to hold a professorial chair at a medical school; she also gave her name to Winifred Cullis School (now Barnwood Park). A great-grandson, Arthur Joseph Cullis, who resided in Barnwood for some time, was the Chief Engineer and Manager of Gloucester Docks, Sharpness New Docks and the Birmingham Navigation Canal in its heyday. By 1900 Joseph had almost fifty descendants in the Gloucester area. The last "Barnwood Cullis", his great-great-granddaughter Dorothy, died at a very good age in 1991.

For much of his adult life, Joseph lived in the Wotton area – in those days very much a part of Barnwood. He became a skilled tradesman and earned a good living as a carpenter. He worked until at least the age of 64 and he kept a ledger noting down the jobs that he did for his customers, the amount he charged for his time and the cost of the wood and nails that he used. Routine work included repairing fences, gates and barns, making furniture, assembling and taking down bedsteads, fitting locks and painting. Amongst his other tasks he included "building two cowhouses", "putting new manger in the stable" and "repairing closehors".

Portraits of Joseph's wife Jane, painted in 1835, and their son Frederick painted in later life. Frederick, who lived until the age of 97, was the son who, as a young man, helped Joseph in his business.

Below is part of a page from his ledger listing some of the work that he did for a Mrs Trimnell in 1835. From this account it is easy to work out that he charged three shillings a day for his labour and half a crown for the services of his son, Frederick, who assisted him.

Towards the end of his life Joseph became ill and, his wife having pre-deceased him, he went to live with his daughter, Jane, in Hucclecote where he died. He was buried on 20th April 1852 in Barnwood churchyard by the vicar, George Escott.

Joseph's will stated that "goods, chattels and credits" were under the value of £20, but the "seven Messuages or tenements, Shops, Garden and other premises" that he left indicated that he had indeed become a very wealthy man.

Browett's Tea Rooms

Nowadays, Budgens stands on the site of what was, before the Second World War, Browett's Refreshment Rooms. During the war W J Lyddiatt, Charles Browett's son-in-law, took over the business. He rebuilt the premises and installed the post office.

The adjacent petrol pumps were rented out to William Maidstone who is shown on the left of the picture below. The gentleman standing next to the vehicle is believed to be Philip Morgan, the owner of the 1933 Austin Light 12/4 Harley. Mr Morgan lived in the large property, called "The Limes", which is still situated up the long drive opposite Budgens.

Tea Room and petrol station, 1946.

In the years after the war "The Limes" became a dog boarding kennels. Meanwhile, and until the 1960s, the café (as it was then frequently called) was used increasingly as a local venue for functions such as wedding celebrations.

Sir Charles Wheatstone

Sir Charles Wheatstone was an inventor and a scientist of international repute; he has always been recognised as Barnwood's most famous son. Although his baptism is recorded in the register of St Mary de Lode, that does not necessarily contradict the long held view that he was baptised at Barnwood in the font which is still in use today. This is because the vicar of Barnwood at that time, Arthur Benoni Evans, was very much involved with both churches and in those days, clergymen sometimes registered births at whichever church was most convenient for them.

As one would expect, there are many long and detailed biographies of Wheatstone which are readily accessible. Francis Harvie Fowler in his *History of Barnwood,* published a century ago, included a brief biography and we have decided to use much of his article here. This seems particularly appropriate as Fowler had met several of Wheatstone's associates. (Fowler probably obtained much of his information from Joseph Stratford's *Gloucestershire Biographical Notes*.)

Fowler wrote "William Wheatstone was a Gloucester tradesman, carrying on a shoemaker's business in a house between College Court and College Street. He married Beata Bubb, a member of an old Gloucestershire family. Her parents, Samuel and Ann Bubb, resided at the Manor House, Barnwood (*pictured on page 44*), and in this old residence Sir Charles Wheatstone, the eminent scientist, was born on February 6th 1802. In 1806 the Wheatstone family removed to London, but Charles probably returned to Barnwood, and passed some part of his early life, including a portion of his school days, with his grandparents. He had a predilection for mathematics and physics. He used to set up automata in the window of the shop which his father kept: these figures, connected by wires with some mysterious apparatus in a room above, went through sundry performances on miniature musical instruments.

In 1828 he invented the Kallidophone, then the Accordion; he was also the inventor of the Stereoscope. For more than a century, investigations and experiments bearing on communication had been carried on in Europe and in America, but to Charles Wheatstone is undoubtedly due the merit of having been the first to render the Electric Telegraph practically available. The invention was patented by him in 1837. He died in 1875."

Fowler added that Wheatstone married at the age of 45, and had two sons and three daughters. One of his sons-in-law, Mr Sabine, is quoted by Fowler as having said "Sir Charles Wheatstone informed me he was born in Barnwood, and that he felt a great interest in an old house there." Apparently, William Rea, an old parishioner whom Fowler knew, recalled that he had bought the Manor House from Mr Bubb, Wheatstone's grandfather. Rea implied that Charles often called to see his old home and that Charles had said that it was the site of some of his earliest experiments.

The article ends with Fowler writing that Wheatstone, on his occasional visits to Barnwood, "would not fail to note the wires running along the Roman road, on which he had scampered as a boy".

The picture of Wheatstone on the left, c1863 is by Antoine Claudet. The picture on the right, by an unknown artist and dated 1876, is called "Scientists". It features some of the major scientific names of the time: left to right we see Michael Faraday, Thomas Henry Huxley, Sir Charles Wheatstone, Sir David Brewster and John Tyndall. The portrait of Wheatstone at the start of this article is by Samuel Laurence and is dated 1868.

(The copyright of each of the three images accompanying this article belongs to the National Portrait Gallery, London. All are reproduced here with its permission.)

Queen Victoria's Diamond Jubilee Celebrations

We have recently celebrated the Diamond Jubilee of Queen Elizabeth II. Only one of our previous monarchs has reached this milestone – Queen Victoria in 1887. So, how was this earlier great event marked in Barnwood?

As was so often the case in those days, it was the local vicar who started the ball rolling. In the March magazine of that year, Francis Harvie Fowler invited letters from parishioners "as to the best method of commemorating the record reign in history". The Parish Council, which had only existed for a little over two years, took up the challenge. They discussed the matter at their April meeting; it was to be the first major function that they were to organise.

Events began with four church services on Sunday 20th June. The day started with the six bells being rung at 7am. During the special "Accession Service" held later in the morning the vicar used as the text for his sermon, 1 Samuel xii verse 24, "be sure to fear the Lord and serve him". The National Anthem was sung and a collection was taken for the benefit of the Gloucester Infirmary.

Later in the week, on Thursday, the bells were again rung; this time at 9am. An hour and a half later 260 children, from both day and Sunday schools, assembled in the school playground and marched to the church. The procession was led by the band of the Gloucester Engineers. After a short service the children processed back to the playground where they were each presented with a Jubilee Medal and a bun. Hearty cheers were given for the donors and then, although it had already been sung earlier in church, another rendition of the National Anthem was heard. As the children dispersed the teachers made their way to Eldonhurst, a large house on the main road, where they were entertained for lunch by Mr & Mrs Holbrook. Mr Holbrook, a generous man who had earlier presented the medals and buns to the children, held several responsible positions in the parish at this time. (He was, incidentally, also in charge of the first drainage scheme to be installed in the parish.)

The chair, for the use of the Chairman of the Parish Council, which Mr Holbrook presented to the parish in 1898.

The afternoon celebrations were held in a large field near the railway bridge, close to what is now Walls roundabout. At the entrance to the field a triumphal arch, decorated in red, white and blue, had been erected. The parish magazine reported that "a meat tea was provided at 3.30pm, in a large tent, for all married people and adults over fifty in Barnwood, Coney Hill, Longlevens and Wotton Without – followed by a tea with cakes and buns for children and those who had not been entertained at the previous meal". The tea tables were tastefully decorated with flowers and an "army of ladies and gentlemen" carried out the carving and waiting. Barrels of beer and perry were available and ginger beer and pickles were also donated by local people – "a large number of whom contributed liberally to the funds". The National Anthem was sung and cheers were given for the numerous organisers. At least 1500 people were present at some stage during the afternoon, including some who recalled the reign of William III.

A programme of sports then took place with prizes awarded for various races. The band played from 5pm until 10pm, during which time dancing and games took place. A firework display followed before the evening drew to a close.

According to Fowler, the "Queen's weather" was enjoyed throughout and he added that "June 24th 1897 will be an ever memorable day in the annals of our village".

Schoolroom 1930

Barnwood School's main classroom was partitioned so that two classes could be taught simultaneously. This photograph, taken in 1930, looks towards the main road. The boy at the far end of the second row from the front is believed to be Wilfred Coopey. Wilfred, a pilot in the RAF, was killed in action during the Second World War. His name appears on the Parish War Memorial.

Walter Wood

Although born in Lancashire, in 1852, Walter Bryan Wood spent most of his life in Gloucester and resided for many years in Barnwood. He lived in Avenue Cottage, the large house which still stands on the main road opposite Barnwood Avenue, with his wife Elizabeth (she was, in fact, his cousin). He was already well connected with the parish as he was related to both Charles Wood, who had been the vicar in the 1840s, and to Alfred Wood who was the first Medical Superintendent at Barnwood House Hospital.

Walter, a freemason, was an accomplished musician and composer and was much involved in the musical life of the city and the Three Choirs Festival.

By profession he was an architect and had worked on the design of many buildings in Gloucester including a number of inns and public houses.

St Catharine's Church in London Road and The High School in Denmark Road were both designed by him. In Barnwood, he was in great demand to plan extensions and alterations to many of the larger houses. His work in the parish also included the design of the Reading Room, opened in 1898, and the War Memorial lych-gate.

Most of his time in Barnwood coincided with the period when Francis Harvie Fowler was the vicar. For over thirty years, these two men did much to improve the social conditions and the quality of life for the residents of the parish. Walter was involved in almost every aspect of parish life. For nearly twenty years he was a churchwarden. He was Chairman of the Parish Council and a Barnwood School Manager (before the days of governors). More unusually, he was the Chairman of the Belgium Refugees Committee and, on occasions, Chairman of the Reading Room Smoking Concerts. For a while he was the church choirmaster and for many years he rang the church bells (he was also President of the Gloucester Ringers).

A generous contributor to many local causes, he hosted fund raising events at his home and both he and his wife made substantial donations to the new free library in the parish. But, perhaps his most unusual gift to Barnwood came at the time when street lighting was a much needed parochial improvement. Walter Wood bought, and erected on the road outside his house, the first street light in the parish.

For many years after his death in 1926, Wood Prizes were awarded by the school from a fund which he had endowed for that purpose. One of the few places where his name may still be seen is on a tablet in the ringing chamber of the church tower.

Barnwood Fête 1922

A picture taken in 1922 at the fête. The Reverend F Paton, vicar, can be seen on the right. Next to him is Walter B Wood, a parishioner who for many years was at the heart of almost everything, both in Barnwood and in the city. On the extreme left of the same row stands A B Evans, the local headteacher.

Mary Cole

Mary Cole, the daughter of a Barnwood butcher, could have become the Queen of England. This fascinating tale starts in the parish and eventually ends here too - but with the unfortunate death of the Vicar of Barnwood.

In March 1767, Mary Cole was born in the Parish of Barnwood. She had two older sisters, Susan and Ann, and a younger brother William. The record of Mary's baptism appears in the register of St Mary de Lode but her brother's baptism is noted in the Barnwood register. It states that "William, son of William Cole and Susannah his wife was baptized (privately) April 4th 1769". Mary's father was described as a respected tradesman who kept The Swan Tavern on the border of Barnwood and Wotton. Apparently, he was also a butcher and he kept a number of grazing animals. When Mary was quite young it seems that the family moved to Wotton-under-Edge where her father died.

By the time she reached sixteen, she was, reportedly, very pretty. So much so, that she caught the eye of Frederick, Lord Berkeley. Although twenty-two years older than she was, this avowed bachelor could not accept that Mary refused to become his mistress. In his *History of Barnwood*, Fowler recalled having had a conversation with a Mr Taylor whose father knew Mary well. Taylor stated that Mary was "an exemplary and virtuous woman who was loved by all her family". He added that on one occasion, when Frederick was Colonel of the South Gloucester Militia and Mary was staying in Gloucester with her sister Ann, Frederick took "a file of men and fired a loud volley of musketry as a ruse" to attract Mary to the window. The discharge fractured "with a crash many panes of glass in the windows, but the amorous Earl cheerfully paid the cost of the damage".

Mary's eventual husband Frederick, the Fifth Earl of Berkeley, dressed in the uniform of the South Gloucester Militia.

The Earl attempted to entrap Mary and her family in various plots in order to try to secure her compliance. A proposal of marriage eventually won her hand and in 1785, at the age of eighteen, she married the Earl at the parish church in Berkeley. But, unbeknown to her, this was a false marriage; it was not properly registered.

In the early days, Mary was probably completely ignorant of her position even though the Earl treated her more like a mistress than a countess. However, as she gave birth to the Earl's children, her influence over his household increased although, by then, she had realised that she was not properly married. During this time Mary and the Earl had seven children but all were registered as illegitimate; her position, both within his household and in society, was anomalous. It was something that troubled her greatly and she frequently raised the subject of a legal marriage with the Earl. He too, had begun to realise the consequences of not having a legitimate heir and the difficulties that he had made for himself. There was little that he could do to alter this; whether he was married or unmarried, his beloved first son could never inherit his title. This inheritance would go to his first legitimate son provided, of course, that he produced one.

And so, on the 6th May 1796 Frederick, the Fifth Earl of Berkeley married Mary Cole, the mother of his children. Before the service Frederick had signed an affidavit stating that there was no lawful impediment to this marriage and that he was a bachelor. Mary Cole was now Mary, Countess of Berkeley, and soon afterwards, she produced the Earl's first legitimate son, Thomas Moreton. But the position of their beloved firstborn, William Fitzhardinge (Fitz), had not changed. When he was born, Mary had believed that she was married and that he was the rightful heir. Both she and the Earl were now becoming increasingly troubled by the conflict that this was causing. One possible solution would be to attempt to prove that the first 'marriage' in 1785 was, in fact, legitimate even though there was no entry in the parish register.

The death of Hupsman, the cleric who had conducted their false marriage ceremony, had removed one obstacle because, at that time, tampering with parish registers was a capital offence and although corrupt, he would never have agreed to alter the records. So, evidence was sought of any documentation that would validate their assertion that a legitimate wedding had originally taken place. Remarkably, the banns and a sheet of paper with the entry of their marriage were found and the Earl started to spread this news in order to legitimise Fitz's position. (It is accepted now that these two documents were forgeries.) But this raised questions about the reason for the second marriage and the veracity of the affidavit that the Earl had made at that time. So much so that when the Earl attempted to put, before the College of Heralds, a proof of descent for his son, there was sufficient disquiet that he was called before the Committee for Privileges at the House of Lords to explain his actions. It did not support his claim.

When eventually the Earl died, in August 1810, matters came to a head. Fitz requested that he, as Earl of Berkeley, be called to Parliament. Again the Committee of Privileges intervened and their proceedings became known as the "Berkeley Peerage Case". The claim was once more rejected. Fitz left London and retreated back to Gloucestershire where he lived as 'Colonel Berkeley'. He died, unmarried and childless, in 1857 following a hunting accident.

Meanwhile Moreton, the first of the legitimate children, who had never expected to become the Sixth Earl, continued to maintain that Fitz had been the rightful heir. The confusion continued for many years and eventually a Second Berkeley Peerage Case was necessary to decide the legitimate heir. And this is when the story returns to Barnwood.

It was in 1891 that the Committee for Privileges at the House of Lords once again looked into the matter of the disputed title. They insisted on examining the parish register of Barnwood to check, for some reason, the entry for the marriage of Mary's sister, Ann. They may also have wished to examine whether or not banns had been called before Mary's "marriage".

William J Kennedy;
Vicar of Barnwood
between 1887 and 1891.

The vicar at the time was the much respected William Kennedy and, as he was the custodian of the registers, he was summoned from his Colin Road vicarage to the Lords. The chances are that he knew several members of the Upper Chamber already, for he was a well connected gentleman. (His son, who on several occasions read the lessons in services at Barnwood Church, was later to become The Right Honourable Lord Justice, Sir William Rann Kennedy, Lord Justice of Appeal.) However, the trip proved fatal for Kennedy because, whilst there on 29th May, he caught the chill which soon developed into the bout of pneumonia from which he died four days later. He was buried in the churchyard at Barnwood.

Footnote. During her marriage, Mary frequently socialised with members of the Royal Family, either in London or at Berkeley. After the death of her husband in 1810, Mary became the focus for the romantic attentions of The Duke of Clarence who was the third son of King George III. The Duke proposed marriage to her in 1811. She wrote to the Duke's brother, The Prince Regent who was then effectively ruling because of the incapacity of his father George III, stating that "she must never entertain such an honour". The Duke went on to become King William IV. Thus, a girl from Barnwood so easily could have become The Queen of England.

(The copyright of the cropped image of Frederick Augustus Berkeley, 5th Earl of Berkeley, by Robert Dighton which accompanies this article belongs to the National Portrait Gallery, London. The image is reproduced here with its permission. The book, Mary Cole: Countess of Berkeley, *written by Hope Costley White and published by G G Harrap in 1961 proved to be an invaluable source during the research of this topic.)*

Barnwood Cycling Club

In the 1880s the pastime of cycling grew in popularity. It gave many people, particularly those who could not afford to keep a horse, their first taste of quick, cheap, independent transport.

But the more moneyed in the population also began to enjoy cycling and many cycling clubs were formed to cater for this leisure activity. The Barnwood club was one of several in the area; it was supported by the vicar and the membership included a number of the more influential residents of the parish. In fact, in 1892 shortly after its formation, Mr Holbrook, a local business man who was secretary of the club, generously took all members out to dinner at the New Inn in Gloucester.

They met on Thursday evenings during the summer months and visited places such as Tewkesbury, Westbury-on-Severn, Newent and Whitminster. The trip up Birdlip Hill and on to Foston's Ash, Bull's Cross, Pitchcombe, Horsepool's Hill, Brookthorpe and home down Church Lane was considered to be one of the more arduous journeys and this, perhaps, explains why "the muster of runners" was only thirteen on that occasion. The party did not return to Barnwood until 11.15pm.

In 1894 the trip to Staunton had to be abandoned "on account of the roughness of the roads". The parish magazine also tells us that in October of that year the Annual Dinner was held jointly with the Barnwood Cricket Club. The venue was the Cross Keys Inn and the cost was one shilling.

A Lantern Parade was organised in 1895. The cyclists met at the Cross Hands, Brockworth, and travelled to Innsworth and then back to Barnwood. Members were congratulated for "the taste which they displayed in decorating their machines".

On one occasion the vicar's wife arranged that "the Girls' Working Party followed the cyclists in a brake". In 1894 a large number of members, together with local dignitaries, assembled "to be immortalised" in a photograph taken by Mr Palfrey of Westgate Street. Although we are told that two good images were taken, sadly, we are unable to obtain a copy.

This picture, taken in 1895, shows two members of the Cullis family, Beatrice and Arthur, on their tandem tricycle. The family had a long association with the parish. It is not known where the photograph was taken.

The History of Barnwood House Hospital

Nowadays, it is difficult to imagine the impact that Barnwood House Hospital, a private mental asylum, had on the parish. Little now remains; we are left with just a few of the peripheral buildings and the memories of those who worked there. Not only did the Hospital cover over 200 acres, but it was also a significant local employer and an important institution at the forefront of the treatment of mental illness.

Its history began around 1800, during a time of enlightenment and change in the care of the mentally sick. Until then, those with mental problems had either been confined to prison or placed in general wards at the Infirmary. The governors of Gloucestershire Infirmary, and others, decided to raise money in order to build an asylum specifically for the care of those suffering from mental illness. One of the Gloucester worthies involved in this activity was the prison reformer Sir George Onesiphorus Paul.

Funds were difficult to obtain and it was not until legislation changed and thereby allowed the County to fund from the rates a lunatic asylum for paupers, that the subscribers were able to undertake a joint venture with the County to open, in 1823, Gloucestershire's first lunatic asylum. This was the Wotton Asylum in Horton Road.

The aim of the subscribers was to ensure that patients received the best care and treatment in an environment to which they were normally accustomed. Payment for these services would be made according to the means of each patient.

However, by 1856, both the subscribers and the County felt that the arrangement at Horton Road did not meet their respective needs. By mutual agreement the County bought out the subscribers who then set about finding an alternative site. It was under the capable management of the chairman at this time, William Henry Hyett from Painswick, that the subscribers found an ideal property nearby: thus they purchased Barnwood House in February 1858.

Barnwood House was originally built as a gentleman's residence in the early years of the 1800s by Robert Morris, who lived nearby in Barnwood Court. Situated on land to the south of the main road, its subsequent owners extended both the house and the lands. In 1838 it was described as "beautifully situated on a lawn fronting to the south commanding extensive views of the adjacent country. It had a greenhouse, walled kitchen garden, and numerous fruit trees and the land occupied some 70 acres".

The front of the building prior to 1896.

Barnwood House Hospital opened as an asylum for 70 patients in January 1860. The two wings of the original building had been extended, one to house male patients and the other female patients. The central block served both as a communal area and as the residence for the Medical Superintendent and his family.

During the following years the building was extended both westward towards Church Lane and eastward towards Upton Lane. Pictures taken at the time show that this extension must have happened in stages, as the need for expansion arose, because the frontage is by no means uniform. Differing roof alignments and variations in style imply that this was a piecemeal development which had probably reached its conclusion by the 1930s.

The front again, but this time after the 1896 rebuild of the central block.

There were four categories of patients and they were housed appropriately. Category Four patients required constant supervision and lived in secure wards at either end of the main building. Category One patients were far less constrained and were able to wander around the grounds and take advantage of the recreational facilities offered.

The Hospital was forever innovative and it was recognised that patients often reached a stage in their treatment when, prior to discharge, they were capable of looking after themselves. Also, ever mindful of the status of many of their patients, the trustees recognised that it was socially more acceptable to some, and to their families, that they were housed in a building that was not called a mental institution. Therefore, in order to develop these philosophies, a number of other buildings were purchased.

North Cottage (now occupied by Emmaus), the Manor House and Lynthorpe were three such local properties.

This large, rather imposing, building was situated on the main road opposite the Reading Room. Called "Lynthorpe", it was originally a private residence. After the closure of the Hospital it was demolished and the site is now occupied by The Church of Latter Day Saints.

Further away, the Hospital acquired Crickley Court, an old coaching inn dating from 1650 and situated at the bottom of Crickley Hill. Opened in 1938, it housed seven ladies and eventually closed about 1958. Seven Springs House (now Sandford School), which was purchased at about the same time, was probably never used as accommodation.

Even further away, and dating from before 1672, was The Wilderness. Purchased by the Hospital sometime before 1884, it housed up to fifteen ladies. Being 900 feet above sea level, and in the Forest of Dean, it offered the Hospital ideal sanatorium conditions. The building closed in 1919 and the ladies were transferred to the Manor House.

Finally, Hume Towers in Bournemouth was purchased in 1954 for use as a seaside holiday home. This fine building, with William Morris stained glass windows, was situated in extensive grounds. It housed up to forty-five patients and offered a welcome respite by the seaside. It closed in 1966.

Hume Towers at Bournemouth.

In the 1930s, the trustees were concerned that the development of factories in Brockworth and the encroachment of both Gloucester and Hucclecote housing were liable to affect the tranquil and rural setting of the Hospital. Therefore plans were made to move to Woodchester Park. Although eleven patients were moved there, and the two farms were managed, this venture was not successful.

Whilst the Hospital continued to expand during the post war years, nationally changes were occurring which would eventually lead to its closure. The fledgling National Health Service with its improving care for those with mental health problems meant that the need for private provision was decreasing. The fact that Barnwood House was "disclaimed" under the National Health Service Act, 1946, and thus remained a private body under the ownership and administration of its governors, merely delayed its inevitable demise.

Barnwood House patients who had the financial resources to meet the fees had always subsidised the less well off patients. But there were now even fewer patients who could afford the costs and income was falling. In only four of the post war years did the total income from patients pay for the cost of their care. The shortfall had to be obtained from other sources, such as dividends from the Hospital's investments. Much of the large building was becoming unoccupied and underutilised.

Another factor that began to exercise the minds of the Hospital's management was the non-contributory pension scheme that had been in existence for many years. The effect of rampant inflation meant that the cost of running this scheme might eventually use up all of the Hospital's capital resources. This problem was resolved by handing over the scheme, plus virtually all the Hospital's investments, to an insurance company.

The combination of both of these financial constraints left no option but to close the Hospital. A two year plan was put into effect to achieve this but, within a few months, it was discovered that the electrical wiring was dangerous and needed replacement. Costing £30,000 (about £500,000 today) this task was completed about six months before the Hospital's closure.

During the two years that it took to close the Hospital, patients were dispersed to their own homes, other hospitals or nursing homes. There were, however, sufficient funds from the sale of land for the Manor House to be converted into a nursing home and eventually nineteen of the remaining patients were transferred there.

The two wings of main Hospital building were demolished soon after its closure and sale in 1968, leaving just the central block which was converted into a private dwelling.

The central block, after the demolition of the wings, seen from a dilapidated tennis court. The houses of Cherston Court are just visible on the right and those of Grovelands on the left.

The land on which the wings were built was sold for housing; Cherston Court and Grovelands being the result. The extensive grounds and fields to the south were also sold for housing although, because of the quality of the trees which had been planted there, the gardens north of the brook became an arboretum. The land immediately to the south of the brook was made into Barnwood Park and a balancing pond.

The end of the 20th century and the end of an era.

During the following years the lands owned by the Hospital to the north of the main road were either sold or leased for industrial development; this area is now known as Barnwood Fields. The financial income from this venture enabled the Trust to continue its charitable works without encumbrance and the Manor House became the focus for the Trust's work.

(Incidentally, the Manor House was offered to the War Office in 1917 as free accommodation with free medical provision for officers suffering from shell shock; the offer was declined.)

44

The Manor House pictured from the south, circa 1950.

The Manor House opened as a nursing home and was intended to be financially independent. It was capable of supporting twenty-three patients to the same high standards of Barnwood House. However, apart from during the first few years, rising costs meant that regular subsidies were required. This situation was not tenable and the decision to close the nursing home and transform it into a day care centre was taken. After some re-equipping and refurbishment, the Manor House opened as such a centre in December 1977, providing facilities for about thirty guests on a daily basis. The initial uptake was low and it was not until the spring of 1979 that numbers started to pick up; then a waiting list opened. Charges were modest and the running costs were subsidised from the Trust's funds. The continuing success of the venture was further enhanced by the construction, in 1981, of a rear annexe in order to provide additional rooms and more facilities.

At this time the Trust embarked on the construction of sheltered housing to complement the work being accomplished in the Manor House.

The stables and outbuildings of the old Manor House were cleared and eighteen, two-bedroom, self-contained bungalows were built on the site. The grounds were landscaped to produce a pleasant and safe environment for the residents.

Having gained experience of running the scheme, the decision was made to construct a further twenty-two dwellings. Completed in September 1986 and built in groups of four, with each opening into a central corridor, these single bedroom units offered an improved level of security and comfort for residents. The new scheme also included an administrative office for the wardens, a common room, two overnight guest rooms, and a suitably equipped bathroom for those residents requiring assistance.

However, by 2010 it was clear that planning for the longer term required further changes to be made. The future of both the Manor Gardens site and of the Manor House has yet to be resolved; this is made more difficult by the fact that the Manor House is a listed building. Fortunately, the Barnwood Trust has an income from the sale of historic land holdings, which means that it does not need to raise money in order to fund its work. It is the intention of the Trust to continue to use this legacy to benefit people with disabilities and mental health challenges in Gloucestershire, thus continuing the vision set out by the original subscribers over 150 years ago.

(Much of the information for the above article was obtained from the histories of the Hospital written by Tom Gale and Bill Church.)

The Hospital from the south west. The farm buildings are on the left and the boiler house and its chimney are at the top of the picture. Barnwood Road runs immediately behind the Hospital buildings.

The back of the Hospital, adjacent to Barnwood Road, showing domestic quarters and, on the extreme left, the head doctor's accommodation. The turret, which was originally used to store water forced by ram from the brook, acted as a lookout for air raids during the Second World War. Parts of the wall next to the pavement remain today.

The Tunnel Under the Road

Whether or not it is still there today we do not know, but underneath Barnwood Road, crossing from north to south and about 30 metres to the east of the pedestrian crossing near Cherston Court, there was once a service tunnel. Just high enough and wide enough for access purposes, it contained the pipes that connected the main building of Barnwood House Hospital to the boiler house. Typical of the concern that the trustees showed for the quality of the environment of its patients, this smoky, somewhat unsightly and industrial necessity was placed well to the north of the Hospital. Supplying domestic hot water, and heating the radiators in the rooms of the main building, were three large boilers. These were initially coal fired but, around 1960, they were replaced by state of the art, oil fired units which meant that the tall, smoke belching chimney, which could be seen for miles around, was demolished.

Part of the laundry building can be seen in front of the boiler house chimney. On the right are the boilers, both old and new.

Before then, the regular maintenance of the chimney was carried out by steeplejacks. It is related that, to reach the top, the steeplejack had to lean backwards for the last ten feet or so, as the chimney widened at this point. Many a challenge was made to the men of the Hospital's maintenance staff to emulate the steeplejacks, but as far as we know, only one ever succeeded in climbing over the top and back down again.

Alongside the boiler house was the laundry, whose machines were powered by the steam from the boilers next door. Washing was brought here from the Hospital, every morning, by handcart. At about the same time another handcart took the Hospital refuse to the incinerator which was situated nearby; half a mile to the north was the cesspit which was the destination for the Hospital's sewage.

As a buffer between these buildings and the main road, the Hospital constructed two hard surface tennis courts. These were surrounded by trees, many of which were unusual species. Today the refurbished tennis courts are still in use and many of the trees still stand.

Even more isolated, on the north side of the road, was the sanatorium. Staffed by a residential matron and several nurses, this was used for the treatment of patients who had infectious diseases. Until the recent construction of the Greenways housing development, the lane leading to this building could still be seen running alongside the site of Barnwood Builders. Adjacent to the sanatorium were the vegetable gardens which kept the Hospital kitchens supplied throughout the year. Typically, the flower gardens were on the south side of the road, next to the Hospital. All of the less attractive features seemed to be on the north side – through the tunnel.

Barnwood House Fire Brigade

During the 1930s there was a rush to reorganise the country's fire fighters. Until this time there had been no nationwide policy and local authorities had made their own arrangements. With the likelihood of a future aerial war increasing, more appliances were manufactured and a number of these were purchased by private organisations wishing to provide their own cover. One such body was Barnwood House Hospital.

The private brigade was manned by volunteers drawn from the staff of the Hospital and they took delivery of a Dennis Trailer Pump on 23rd June 1937. It cost the princely sum of £636 and was stored in the Hospital garage. Formerly the stables, this building can still be seen on Barnwood Road almost opposite Cherston Court, and is easily recognised by its clock tower. Duties included protecting the Hospital and training the nursing staff to cope with fires.

The new crew did not have to wait long for their first emergency call. It came on 26th August 1937 when a hay rick caught fire. The incident took place in a field behind Avenue Cottage, which still stands on the main road opposite Barnwood Avenue. In those days this land formed part of the Hospital farm.

The crew pulled and pushed the pumping appliance down Barnwood Road as fast as they could. But, it was unbalanced and so they persuaded a 10 year old lad to sit on the pump and act as ballast. John Morris took little persuading. Over seventy years later he recalled the occasion and remembered the excitement. The Brigade log book reports being "called out at 4.20pm". Water was "pumped from a disused gravel pit at 110 lbs per square inch for half an hour. Hayrick controlled and fire prevented from spreading to barn nearby". The emergency was resolved "by 5.30pm and 550 feet of hose was used".

A somewhat amusing incident happened that afternoon. A well-known local gentleman went to watch the new brigade in action and some of his comments directed towards the crew became offensive; he was put in his place by a well-aimed jet of water from the hose!

Such call outs were rare. The crew spent the war years supervising the Hospital air raid shelters and, night after night, taking the pump engine to the brook (now in Barnwood Park) beyond the Hospital and laying out the hoses for the anticipated air attack. Fortunately, it never came; the nearest bomb fell a few hundred yards away from the Hospital.

After the war, the crew took delivery of a new appliance. A Sulzer pump engine, mounted on a Fordson 7V Heavy Unit, was received from the National Fire Service on 22nd July 1946. The Barnwood House Brigade enlisted with the Auxiliary Fire Service (AFS) and, for a while at least, one of the Bedford Green Goddesses was entrusted to their care. By this time the emphasis was on Civil Defence training as the nation prepared itself for the possibility of a nuclear attack. Fire drill no longer took place at the Hospital but at the fire station on Barnwood Road and later at Eastern Avenue. The crew regularly practised at the docks on the fire launch "Salamander" and competed as an AFS team in fire service competitions.

Coincidentally, both the Hospital and the AFS ceased to exist in 1968 – the former because of financial difficulties, the latter because of the receding risk of nuclear attack. The Fordson, sadly, was sold at auction together with the rest of the crew's equipment in June 1968 when the Hospital closed.

This significantly repaired picture shows the Barnwood House crew in the mid 1950s, after they had joined the AFS, standing in front of the Fordson. The words "Trustees of Barnwood House" can be deciphered on the side of the appliance. The two men on the extremes are instructors from the AFS; the central six are from the Hospital. Left to right they are Tom Morgan, Wilf Halliday, Cliff Porter, Bill Morris, Ron Baldwin and Charlie McBurnie.

On the "Salamander" at Gloucester Docks.

Ross Ashby

Ever since it opened in 1860, Barnwood House Hospital had always been at the forefront of research into treatments for mental illness. But its most active period in this field was during the middle years of the 20th century. Much of the work was undertaken during the twelve years that Doctor Ross Ashby, a deep and original thinker, was Director of Research at the Hospital.

William Ross Ashby, a Londoner, was born in 1903. After completing his schooling in Edinburgh he attended Cambridge University. Eventually, he became a psychiatrist and a pioneer in cybernetics. Although he did not find writing easy he published two books, "An Introduction to Cybernetics" and "Design for a Brain", both of which were widely regarded. He worked at a number of hospitals including St Bartholomew's in London. It was in 1947, after serving in India with the Royal Army Medical Corps, that he came to Barnwood.

Initially, as a biochemist, he was employed to investigate the enzymes involved in electro-convulsive therapy (often referred to as ECT or electric shock treatment). This process had been invented in Italy in 1938 and was first used in the UK, at Barnwood House, a year later when it was trialled on five patients. In 1941, the Hospital became the first institution to use leucotomy as a treatment. As Director of Research, Ashby was very much involved in the development of these techniques. In his spare time, he built his "thinking machine" using four ex-RAF bomb control units, valves and liquid-filled, magnetically-driven potentiometers. He called this machine "The Homeostat".

Ross Ashby with the "Homeostat".

The invention certainly created worldwide interest. It was a very heavy machine and the most advanced of its kind. In January 1949, *Time* magazine quoted Ashby as saying "it is the closest thing to a synthetic human brain so far designed by man".

Ross enjoyed listening to jazz; he was also interested in photography and astronomy. He painted with water colours – a skill he developed after finding himself in India without a camera. He was a competent repairer of clocks and watches and whilst at Barnwood House he willingly aided those whose timepieces had malfunctioned. Occasionally, he became so preoccupied with his work that, according to the person who delivered his daily lunch to the laboratory, he would forget to eat his meal. He was regarded by contemporaries at the Hospital as a friendly gentleman who encouraged and assisted students.

The laboratory where Ashby worked. The building was once a games room. Part of the Grovelands development now stands upon this site.

After leaving Barnwood he worked in America and became a professor at the University of Illinois. In 1964 he was invited to Russia in order to spend the money that his Russian edition of "Design for a Brain" had earned. (In those days transferring money across borders was not straightforward.) Because of the political situation, his wife did not accompany him - but he bought her a fur coat. Unfortunately, she never wore it because it was designed for the harsher Russian winters. Ross Ashby died in 1972.

(The copyright of the two photographs of Ross Ashby belongs to The Estate of W Ross Ashby; the photographs are reproduced here with its permission. We are grateful to have been allowed to quote from the website www.rossashby.info).

The Italian Connection

Ever since it opened, Barnwood House had always enjoyed stability in its staffing. Even during wartime, because of the national system for reservation of certain occupations, very few of the Hospital's staff were actually away on military service. Nevertheless, by the late 1940s, retirements and the availability of more attractive employment opportunities elsewhere, particularly for women, meant that there was quite a large turnover of staff. Although accommodation (there were over thirty houses on the estate) was available for maintenance staff and full board in the main building was granted to both nurses and "domestics", recruitment became an issue. No longer could the local area supply all those needed and so, like many other organisations throughout the land, the Hospital began to look further afield. Four kitchen staff came from Iceland and a good many more from Italy. These female workers were only allowed to remain at the Hospital so long as they were single. But it was a good life; they were well looked after and they ate the same high quality food as the patients.

During the 1950s and 1960s many foreign nationals were employed. But, of course, these workers were subject to UK immigration procedures. Typical of the domestic staff working at the Hospital was Lucia Rubicco. She was born in Pietradefusi in southern Italy and came to the UK in 1960. Initially, she was given permission to stay for 12 months and her presence was subject to her reporting for work at Barnwood House.

Lucia worked in the kitchens under the supervision of Lena French, who was Head Cook for almost 30 years. Whilst at the Hospital Lucia married a Ukrainian which, of course, meant that she lost her post at the Hospital. Like many other foreign domestics she remained in the United Kingdom; indeed some of the Italian staff and their families still live in Gloucester.

Lucia before leaving Barnwood House for her wedding at St Peter's Church. On her right is the Head Cook, Lena French, and on her left is the Hospital Matron, Anne MacMillan. Miss French and Miss MacMillan were well known in Barnwood and were invited to be the judges of the Parish Coronation competitions in 1953.

Winter 1962, enjoying the novelty of snow; the Italian domestic staff outside the Hospital in Barnwood Road.

Memories of Barnwood House Hospital

The history of the Hospital is told elsewhere; here we look at what it was like to live and work there. Many stories and anecdotes have been related; some can be told now, others will have to wait a little longer.

Right from the outset, both the comfort and care of the patients (some of whom were household names) were considered in every detail; welfare was of paramount importance. The main building had been converted from a gentleman's residence and was situated in a large expanse of land, much of which had been laid out as pleasure gardens including several tennis courts and a croquet lawn.

An early picture of the croquet lawn.

There were a number of pathways around the extensive grounds. One, known as the Ladies' Walk, went around the periphery and was about a mile long, crossing the Wotton Brook via two footbridges.

The brook ran through the grounds and widened into a small lake, which was held back by a weir and sluice gates, before the outflow ran under Church Lane. The lake, home to a number of swans, was never really deep enough to make drowning easy but, nevertheless, it was a target for a number of patients who had to be unceremoniously removed from its muddy waters.

The sluice gates around 1970.

A stone built summer house and a rock garden offered patients a tranquil moment amongst the trees. Many of the trees had been brought there from abroad by patients' relatives; a number of these trees still remain today in the Barnwood Arboretum.

The summer house.

Some 12 gardeners were employed to maintain the lawns and flowerbeds. Unexpected hazards often beset these men for it is told that, on one occasion when the lawnmower was being used, a naked female patient ran and lay down in front of the machine. Unperturbed, the gardener gently lifted the lady to one side and carried on mowing only to be faced with the same obstruction a few moments later! Attendants were soon on the scene, the lady was removed, and the gardener continued on his way.

Attendants and servants were required to ensure that any patient in their care did not run away. The cost of "retaking such a patient" would be deducted from their wages.

Being a private institution, managed by a board of trustees, patients were expected to pay for their accommodation and treatment. However, admission was based solely on social position and mental condition, and not on the ability to pay. Thus, patients were subsidised provided that they "possessed so much education and refinement as would cause them to feel the loss of comfortable surroundings" if they were to be sent to less luxurious accommodation. "They must, from want of means, be unable to pay the ordinary rate and their mental condition must be such as to show a reasonable prospect of recovery."   Preference for financial assistance was given to those patients who came from, or were associated with, the County of Gloucestershire.

Extensions to the building eventually allowed for up to 160 patients. However, the numbers fluctuated and the 1881 census records that there were 145 patients consisting of 63 men and 82 ladies. Their ages ranged from 18 to 91. The majority of ladies were "living on their own means", but only about a third of the men were so recorded.

For most of the time staffing levels were sufficient. Only during the two world wars did the Hospital have some slight difficulties. In 1935, the 151 patients were looked after by 72 nurses, both male and female, who worked unusually long hours. There were also attendants and servants who looked after the patients' needs. Supporting them inside the house were cooks, housemaids, parlour maids, pantry maids, pantry boys, porters and a footman. Outside, there was the maintenance team of artisans, labourers and gardeners. The farm employed some half dozen hands.

The nursing staff at an early, but unknown, date.

The gardeners, again at an early date.

Great efforts were made to ensure that the patients had entertainment and suitable leisure. For the men there was a skittle alley, billiards and snooker and the male members of staff were encouraged to participate with the patients in playing these games.

The billiard room and the skittle alley.

A cricket team, formed of staff and patients, played regularly during the season on the cricket pitch behind the chapel. Visiting teams needed to be sympathetic to the difficulties of playing against a team of patients several of whom could be pedantic in their approach to the game.

To ensure that a fair balance of skills was maintained, the Hospital team was often supplemented by players from outside the Hospital who received a small payment for their services. The ladies could watch and enjoy the proceedings from the comfort of a nearby pavilion, a safe distance away from the occasional six.

A view from the cricket pitch with the cricket pavilion on the left, the chapel in the centre and a sight screen on the right.

Inside the building there was a dance hall whose teak-lined floor and wide stage allowed for numerous entertainments and events. There were regular concerts and lectures. Twice weekly, a film was shown. This was punctuated with music from a piano as the reels were changed on the single projector. Before the advent of television, amateur dramatics were popular and one can imagine many a thespian treading these boards hoping for stardom. Local choirs frequently visited to entertain both staff and patients.

The dance hall was also used for concerts and as a cinema.

Whenever there was a dance in the hall, the band or the orchestra would be installed on the stage, secreted behind tall flowers and vegetation; it would be heard rather than seen. Once a year, a special dance was given as a reward to the staff for all their hard work. Traditionally the first dance was led by the Medical Superintendent and the Matron. Today, those who were there at the time readily recall the grandeur of the occasion. Typical of the age, the Hospital was very aware of the hierarchy of its staff who were expected to maintain their station both in their work and in their social relationships. One story is told of a member of staff who, when it was discovered that he intended taking to a dance his lady friend who was "only" a parlour maid, was told in no uncertain terms that this was inappropriate and that he was not to attend.

The Hospital had its own farm, with cattle, poultry, pigs and cornfields. This was capable of supplying most of the Hospital's needs and, along with its extensive market garden and greenhouses, the Hospital was able to maintain its culinary standards throughout the deprivations of the Second World War. During the 1950s, the farm supplied two churns of fresh milk every morning and another two in the evening; each churn held ten gallons. Ten dozen eggs were delivered to the kitchen every day by the poultry man. A gallon of fresh cream was also supplied on a daily basis. Special occasions were acknowledged with the occasional treat, for example a number of geese would be delivered for Michaelmas.

The kitchens, located underground, were large and well equipped. During the 1950s and 1960s the majority of cooks were Italians from Milan and were managed by the Kitchen Superintendant, Miss Lena French, a firm Scot.

The cooks lived in the block above the kitchens and, on hot summer days, could be seen leaning out of the windows chatting to each other in true Mediterranean style.

Kitchen staff at work c1960.

The coach house and stable block housed, in the early days, two horses and a carriage. These were used to take patients out for excursions.

The stable block, c1910; its appearance has changed little in over a century.

However, in 1920 two motor cars were purchased. A daily routine then developed, whereby some patients were taken on a country drive or a shopping expedition in the morning and others were driven out in the afternoon. By the late 1950s, two Daimlers belonging to the Head Doctor were housed there too.

The Hospital employed a pageboy who, properly attired in his uniform, met important guests and visitors at the main entrance. Here, in a room to one side of the hallway, was the Hospital's posting box, a wooden upright chest containing a sack which was emptied daily. One postman recalled the quality and style of this piece of utilitarian furniture. He related how several of the patients would stand and watch him empty the box, something he found rather unsettling. All parcels and letters to and from the patients had to be submitted for inspection.

However, it was more difficult to monitor gifts bought in by visitors. A story is told that on one occasion a patient became unwell after eating the chocolates brought in by her visiting husband. A month after being discharged from the Hospital she died and was buried. A later exhumation of the body revealed the presence of arsenic. Her husband was subsequently found guilty of murder and thus "Armstrong the Poisoner" became the only solicitor in the history of England to be hanged for murder.

The majority of patients had their own bedroom, although there were a few dormitories for those who could not afford single accommodation. Each room had a fireplace and there were supplementary central heating radiators. In the early days water from the Wotton Brook, which ran through the grounds, was pumped by rams up to cisterns on the roof in order to give the Hospital its own water supply. Sewage went into two cesspits some considerable distance away to the north.

A dormitory.

An occupational therapy room offered classes in weaving and basket making. Physical exercises and Morris dancing also took place there. This large room, overlooking the gardens, had a beautiful curved ceiling which, we are reliably informed, took ten gallons of paint to cover.

The occupational therapy room.

Nursing and domestic staff lived in the Hospital alongside the patients and therefore their accommodation was better than that of many others in similar occupations. They ate what the patients ate. "If salmon was in season then we ate salmon, if it was pheasant, then we ate pheasant", related one domestic. Domestics wore blue and white uniforms in the morning and black and white after lunch, when visitors were welcomed and escorted to the patients.

From the early days, staff responsibilities towards the care of patients were clearly laid out in the Hospital's Rule Book. Typical of the tone was the introduction, with staff being reminded that "patients suffered from a disease and were therefore to be pitied and not blamed. They must be treated with the same respect as if they were of sound mind and at liberty". There were over 50 rules laying out the duties and responsibilities for the Head Attendants, Night Attendants, Ordinary Attendants and Servants. At the end, written in red, were the penalties and fines incurred for breaking these rules.

The day started early. Head Attendants visited all the rooms in their departments by seven o'clock, when the night staff handed over to the day staff. This ensured that the attendants and nurses were up and fulfilling their duty, that bedroom windows were opened and patients were washed and neatly dressed ready for breakfast.

Morning prayers were then said, after which there was a daily inspection. All newspapers and periodicals were changed and the rooms cleaned and tidied.

Grace was said at mealtimes. Patients were allowed wine and this was recorded in the "Wine and Diet book". Attendants were required to "neatly lay out the tables at mealtimes", cutlery and glasses were to be "clean and bright and carefully counted and locked up after each meal".

There was strict segregation between the sexes. Female patients occupied the east wing, male patients the west. Attendants of one sex could not enter the living areas of the other unless duly instructed to do so.

At dusk during the winter and at 9pm in the summer, all external doors were locked. The night staff came on duty at 9pm. Evening prayers were followed by a general locking of internal doors preparatory to all patients being settled down by 10pm. Every effort was made to ensure that night time was quiet and orderly. Doors and windows were secured on windy nights to stop rattling and the staff had to wear shoes that did not make a noise on the floors. At night, special attention was given to the care of epileptic or suicidal patients in order to ensure that they were safe.

There was, however, a darker side to life in the Hospital. Although not common, suicides were not unknown. A tale is related by a former member of staff who was getting married and therefore had to seek employment elsewhere. Barely two hours before being interviewed for her new job she discovered a patient hanging in a cupboard. Despite the shock she still attended the interview!

A long service tunnel ran underground from one end of the main building to the other. It was wide enough and tall enough to allow staff, goods and services to freely and rapidly move from one part of the Hospital to another, although attendants were only allowed to use it at mealtimes. The chapel was in regular use; all attendants and servants who could sing were expected to attend to form the choir.

The Hospital Chapel, now a weight training centre.

Staff were not allowed to smoke inside the building and they were expected to be sober and well-attired at all times. Indeed, a picture of the maintenance team clearly shows the majority wearing jackets and ties.

The maintenance staff in the late 1950s.

As well as a private telephone exchange which serviced the whole of the Hospital and its outbuildings, there was also a 'state of the art' fire alarm system which was connected to the nearby residences of all key members of the staff.

But today the main building, the farm and many of the ancillary buildings are gone. Newcomers to the area drive along the Barnwood Road and pass the remains of the boundary wall without knowing anything of the style of life which existed on the other side, less than half a century ago.

And the number of people who do remember is getting fewer!

Christmas at the Hospital

A Christmas card from the Hospital. The photograph is taken from what is now Barnwood Park.

Christmas at Barnwood House was always well celebrated. Each ward would have its own very tall Christmas tree which had been supplied from the Hospital grounds. It was tastefully decorated and was the focus of the ward party. Staff, and children from the estate, were invited to these occasions and, indeed, encouraged to attend as it was considered beneficial to the patients' wellbeing. A big cake would be cut and delicacies would be offered on large silver trays. Crackers would be pulled and the ward sister would deliver a short seasonal message. The event would be over by late afternoon, although the same guests would inevitably meet up the next day at another similar function.

As Christmas approached, the choir from Hucclecote Parish Church attended in order to entertain the patients. A former chorister recalled that "we changed into our cassocks and surplices in a billiard room just off the main corridor. We were then ushered into a large hall and went through our repertoire of carols. I can remember feeling rather apprehensive when faced with rows of residents some of whom did seem rather different to the norm and displayed some odd behaviour. However, this was all made well worthwhile when we were each given half a crown for our efforts. It seemed like a lot of money to us in those days. My overriding memory of the place was of rather splendid decor and fittings, with lots of very high ceilings and highly polished wood."

Barnwood Church choir sang in the main hallway and corridors every Christmas.

Another chorister, this time from Barnwood Parish Church choir, recounted that "On Christmas Eve, the older boys and the men always went carol singing. The ritual was the same every year. We called at the large houses in the parish, sang two carols, a donation for the choir outing fund was placed in the tin, another carol was sung and then we were offered a drink. By the time the last call was made, always at Barnwood House, some of the men were in really good voice. At the Hospital we never saw any patients; we were led down several wide and well furnished corridors and sang in hallways close to open doors. The sound travelled well and the nursing staff seemed to appreciate it. We were always on our best behaviour; it was clearly expected and the place had the sort of atmosphere where everyone felt obliged to behave anyway. But it was really Christmassy, singing around the Christmas trees."

Some of the domestic and nursing staff enjoy Christmas lunch together in 1962. Matron is in the centre of the picture.

It was a very busy time for both nurses and domestic staff with little time off and much rushing around. But they were well rewarded with a "magnificent Christmas Dinner" as one former member of staff described it. She added "and you could help yourself to as much as you wanted, for over the Christmas period we were really fed well; food was very, very available". Indeed it was; fifty Norfolk Black turkeys were supplied by the farm and, for those for whom turkey meat had little appeal, a couple of dozen capons. The estate also produced hams for special meat teas, and there was fresh cream aplenty to top the sweet course as the cows were, understandably, still milked at Christmas.

Doris Warren

It was in 1928 that Miss Bullock, a young woman from Woolaston, near Lydney, completed her training and arrived at Barnwood School (in those days situated on Barnwood Road) to teach infants. Her job entailed working in a rather small room containing eighty children. Whilst half of the class sat at clumsy old fashioned desks to work, the other half sat on the floor to read. In those days a notebook was hung on the headteacher's door and each teacher was expected to sign the book in the morning, noting their arrival time, and again in the evening with the time of their departure. Furthermore, the teacher on duty was expected to note the condition of the toilets (buckets in those days), the cloakrooms and the playground. Miss Bullock recalled that on one occasion, when everything was satisfactory, she wrote "Sat all day". The headteacher sent for her and reprimanded her explaining that she "was not employed to sit all day".

The headteacher concerned was Mr A B Evans who had been employed at Barnwood since the end of the 19th century. He retired in 1932. Miss Bullock recalled that Mr Wager, the new headteacher, introduced a school uniform with a badge reading "Respice Finem" meaning "Look to the End". In the summer of 1933 a new wooden building was erected away from the main school. This became the infant department.

By now Miss Bullock was well-established. She always appeared smartly dressed, wearing a tie and a blouse underneath a suit. Her pupils used slates and chalk for their work and, at the end of the day, whilst sitting round the old stove, the class always sang a hymn or a lullaby; "Now the Day Is Over" was a favourite. She is remembered by pupils of the time as being kind but strict and "a very good teacher who taught everyone to read and write". One particular pupil recalled being given a jar of beads and some thread to keep her happily occupied on her first day at school.

Apparently, there were suitors in those early days; a boyfriend on a motorcycle is remembered by former pupils. Until 1938 children from Longlevens were educated at Barnwood. Then a new school was built in Longlevens and Mr Wager left to be in charge there. Mr Harris, the new headteacher, was much admired by eligible young women in the parish. One of the School Managers (governors were not to see the light of day for another half century) suggested to Miss Bullock that she was perhaps eligible herself. She dismissed the idea saying "One teacher in our family is enough!"

On September 3rd 1939 war was declared. On the previous day the school staff had awaited the arrival of evacuees. No time was lost in digging trenches in the school garden (to the east of what is now the Deaf Community Centre) in which to house shelters for the children during the expected air raids. The school, after the summer break, did not reopen until the end of September by which time the shelters had been completed. Gas mask drill and air raid drill were both included in the daily timetable. Miss Bullock recalled "It could be quite frightening in the shelters when enemy aircraft passed over. The most frightening afternoon was when Derby Road was bombed. I had just dismissed my infants when the sirens sounded and the bombs dropped. I gathered together as many of the little ones as I could and hurried into the shelter allotted to the infants".

Miss Bullock supervises the infants for air raid practice in 1939 whilst Mr Harris, the headteacher, looks on.

During the war, with Mr Harris on active service, Mrs V M C Smith took over as headteacher and she, together with Miss Bullock, formed a Youth Movement Group which was devoted to knitting for the troops and camouflaging army uniforms. For her war service, Miss Bullock also did regular voluntary work at one of the Gloucester railway stations where she spent her evenings brewing and distributing tea and coffee to the servicemen who were passing through the station. After the war she was awarded The Defence Medal by the Home Office.

In 1942, for the first time, cooked lunches were supplied to pupils at the cost of 5d each. There were no dining or kitchen facilities in the school and so the lunches were cooked in Longlevens and then transported to Barnwood. The Bowling Club Pavilion, which was on the opposite side of the road from the school, was used as the dining room. This practice continued until the school came under City Council control, some 25 years later, when a kitchen was built as an extension to the school building.

Towards the end of the war children from Brockworth and Hucclecote started to attend the school. This was partly because of its popularity and partly because there was no school in Brockworth. Miss Bullock was put in charge of transport and it was her duty to cross pupils over the busy main road to catch the buses home. At Barnwood Church, in the early 1950s, Miss Bullock married Bill Warren, one of the bus drivers.

Mrs Warren continued to be in charge of the infants. Reading, writing, arithmetic and spelling were all taught with real enthusiasm. Early each autumn she would begin to make crackers for the annual Christmas party. She was also responsible for producing all school notices, which she did with the old fashioned printing jelly that predated both the Banda machine and the photocopier.

Crossing to the Bowling Club's pavilion for the Christmas party in 1954. Mrs Warren and Mr Morgan are helping Father Christmas. It is just possible to read "Gloucestershire CC" on the crossing board. Barnwood was not in the city at this time.

In 1959 Mrs Warren became the deputy headteacher. Mrs Smith had already retired by this time and two more headteachers quickly came and went – one due to ill health and the other for personal reasons. In 1962 Mr G R Parry was installed as the headteacher; he was the seventh, and last, head with whom Mrs Warren worked.

A period of sustained and necessary stability followed over the next ten years. Prize days, sports days and summer fêtes became part of the annual calendar; Christmas parties and nativity plays came and went; Father Christmas remembered to visit the infants every year – although Mr Etheridge no longer always occupied the sleigh! A new classroom was built and Mrs Warren moved in with "my infants". But there was one more major challenge to accomplish. She was given the task of organising a reunion to celebrate the school centenary.

Doris Warren celebrating 40 years in the classroom.

She spent the summer holiday of 1973 trying to trace former pupils (she'd taught most of them!) and in January of the following year a grand reunion was held at the Mercers Hall. Writing afterwards, Mrs Warren wrote "Old and young were there reminiscing. A couple who started courting in the Infant Department were celebrating their diamond wedding at the time. Mr Parry and I gave speeches and the Rev M O Seacome extended a warm welcome to all". A Centenary Service, held in church the following Sunday, was well-attended with people travelling from considerable distances. Five days later the children held their Thanksgiving Service. Centenary mugs, designed by Michael Seacome and made by the monks at Prinknash Abbey, sold very quickly at 85p each. The success of the celebration served as a testament to the organisational skills of Mrs Warren.

Six months later, in July 1974, Doris Warren retired – "not from choice but because retirement age had caught up with me. I was sad having to leave my beloved school after over 46 years. The school had become part of me, my second home. I had a wonderful send off".

Mrs Warren's retirement dinner, July 1974. From left to right, Reverend Michael Seacome, Mrs Doris Warren, Mr Bill Warren, Dr Mary Seacome, Mr G R Parry.

Having worked with both A B Evans and Betty Nelmes, Doris Warren had colleagues who taught at Barnwood in three different centuries. After retirement she continued as a loyal member of St Lawrence Church where, for many years, she was treasurer. She received the Citizen of Gloucester Award for services to Gloucester Royal Hospital League of Friends, the Royal British Legion and Barnwood Parish Church.

Some years after her death, the garden of remembrance in the churchyard was constructed in her memory.

(The above account is based on the recollections of former pupils and colleagues and on the memories, which she wrote several years after her retirement, of Doris Warren herself.)

Harry Godwin Chance Memorial

This was once one of the more interesting memorials in the churchyard. It is situated just to the west of the church porch, although now it is in a much dilapidated state. The stone, shaped like a propeller, marked the grave of Harry Godwin Chance who, for almost forty years from the end of the 19th century, was connected with *The Citizen*. He was, for some time, both editor and proprietor. Harry Godwin Chance was very active in local music circles and was a founding member of the Gloucester Rotary Club. He died in 1932 and was buried here in Barnwood. The memorial stone on his grave was, however, erected in memory of his son Eric who, as a member of the Royal Air Force, was killed in action in Italy during the First World War and buried abroad. The photograph below shows The Reverend M O Seacome and The Reverend A J Holloway, the Diocesan Director of Education, walking beside the memorial, following the Barnwood School Centenary Service in 1974.

Christmas 1951

Despite ration books still being required for most shopping trips, by Christmas 1951 the nation was being encouraged to try to lift itself out of the post war gloom which still prevailed. So Barnwood tried – and it tried hard!

In November, the main assembly room in Wotton Hall had been "transformed into an enchanting fairyland of light, colour and brightness" as "brisk business" took place at the Christmas Fair. The parish magazine also said that "stalls selling decorations, produce, flowers, things eatable, old books and tinned goods" were prominent. The school provided a Christmas tree, the scouts ran the sideshows, the Mothers' Union served teas and the Young Wives entertained the gathering with songs. Mr Etheridge, proprietor of the Grove Crescent corner shop, was the auctioneer for the afternoon. The sum of £125 was raised for the church at this, Barnwood's first Christmas Fair.

There were several events at the school that Christmas. Parents and friends spent "a most enjoyable afternoon listening to carols" sung by the pupils and there were two parties for the children. The infants had made hats and crackers for their celebration, which was attended by Father Christmas who arrived on a fire engine. He was greeted by a fairy (Rosemary Knight) and her prince. He presented each child with a picture book from the tree and a cracker filled with sweets. Everyone "enjoyed a wonderful tea".

At their party, the older children were entertained by a Punch and Judy show, a cowboy act with magic and some "talkie films including Cinderella". It was common in those days for countries like Canada and Australia to try to give a little festive cheer to the United Kingdom. Consequently, it came as no surprise – but was still a gesture none the less appreciated – when the "people of Australia sent two tins of dried fruit for each child so that their families might have some Christmas delicacies".

On Christmas Day the 138 communicants were able to choose between services at midnight, 8am and noon. Other worshippers were able to attend either matins at 11am or evensong at 6.30pm. The new altar linen, presented by the Mothers' Union, was used for the first time that day. A carol service had taken place the previous Sunday.

The weather on Christmas Eve may have deterred some from attending the midnight service but there was a good turn out from the choir who, together with Mr Williams the organist, were congratulated on the quality of the music.

Early in the New Year, two Sunday School parties were held. "Fifty infants sat down to a splendid tea in Wotton Hall" and were entertained by a nativity play presented by the Mothers' Union. The juniors watched "a splendid film show". In mid-January, again at Wotton Hall, the annual Parish Christmas Social took place. As usual this much anticipated event was thoroughly enjoyed by all.

Perhaps, however, the most important event for the parish that Christmas was the fitting of electric lighting in the whole of the school building (two classrooms had been fitted the previous term). This "long-felt need" was installed whilst the school was closed for the holidays.

The Barnwood Festival

In May 1965, with the trees in the Avenue in full blossom, the first Barnwood Festival took place. This festival of arts was centred on the church. It was the brainchild of the vicar, Michael Seacome, who was himself a painter, a musician and a magician. For the next 25 years this annual event contributed significantly to the cultural life of the city. It gave pleasure to many, and involved a large number of people who participated in a variety of ways, whether as performers, committee members, helpers, sponsors or as members of an audience. According to its founder, the objective of the event was to encourage cultural skills whilst "emphasising the spiritual nature of such activities within the church of the 20th century".

Although the vast majority of events took place in the parish church, the occasional large concert or entertainment was held elsewhere, whilst the annual art exhibition was housed in the home of Michael and Mary Seacome.

Many local performers, both amateur and professional, featured in the programmes and these entertainers were complemented by professional artists from afar. One of these, comedian Cyril Fletcher, a household name of the time, remarked on the "hilarious warmth of the audience". Harry Gabb, once organist of the Chapels Royal, commented favourably on the quality of the Barnwood organ saying that it was a "small but superb instrument, perfectly designed for the building".

Every year there were lectures, talks and recitals. On different occasions there were competitions for bell ringers, photographers and writers. Sometimes a classic film was shown and frequently there was a dramatic production. Well-known stars of the day such as Joyce Grenfell, Joseph

Cooper and David Kossoff appeared as, indeed, did Vercoe the Clown. There was always a festival service with a well-known preacher.

By 1989, the organisers were getting older, Michael Seacome had retired and the future was somewhat uncertain. The committee announced that it wished "to go out on a high". This wish was fulfilled and the Festival ceased after seeing both serious and popular entertainment flourish for a quarter of a century, thanks to the vision and enterprise that inspired it.

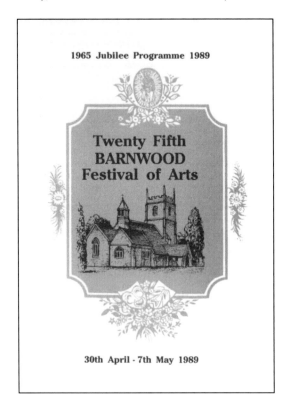

The cover of the final Barnwood Festival programme.

Ringing in the Mayor

In May 1974, after Harry Worrall had been installed as Mayor of Gloucester, the Barnwood Ringers rang a quarter peal of Grandsire Triples as a celebration. Although Harry Worrall was a bell ringer at St Mary de Lode, the quarter was rung at Barnwood because Michael Seacome was The Mayor's Chaplain. With the Barnwood Ringers are, in the centre of the group left to right, The Reverend Michael Seacome, The Mayor of Gloucester, Les Barry (captain of Gloucester Cathedral Ringers) and The Mayoress.

Barnwood Scouts – The Early Years

As early as 1920, several Barnwood boys had availed themselves of the invitation to join the scout troop in St Catharine's Parish. A few years later, towards the end of the 1920s, there had been a scout troop and a cub pack in Barnwood, but this venture was not really successful and both the pack and the troop ceased to exist not long after starting.

It was in October 1936 that the new vicar, Canon Eric Noott, wrote in the parish magazine that he wished to inform "all boys over the age of 10 years connected with Church or Sunday School that a scout group is to be formed". He invited them to make contact with him or with Mr Chapman, the new scoutmaster. The first meeting was held in the Institute (now called the Reading Room) on October 6th when three patrols were established. Thus, it was that in November Canon Noott wrote "the old 11th Gloucester Barnwood Troop has been reformed and is now attached to the Parish Church". It was to remain a church sponsored group for thirty years.

On November 22nd the church was packed for the enrolment of the first twelve "to have formed the Barnwood Parish Church Troop". They were R Andrews, J Bleackley, G Cook, J Davies, D Dawe, G Kerr, R Maidstone, D Spencer, F Tredgett, R Tredgett, L Venn and R Venn.

In December the scouts were very grateful to receive, from a kind donor, the gift of a troop flag. Within the year, Miss Marks and Miss Mitchell were running a Wolf Cub Pack. The Barnwood Scouts were going well - but war was fast approaching.

At the Troop's third birthday party in November 1939, the scouts were joined by the boys from Birmingham who had been billeted in the parish. Local scout leaders were being called up and, with blackouts and rationing, it was almost impossible to continue normally. A small group of the Barnwood lads formed a War Service Patrol, helping with the war effort in any way that they could. The few camps that they did have were at Ullenwood where they were often disturbed by the anti-aircraft firing, from around the hills, which was protecting the Gloucester Aircraft Factory.

BOY SCOUTS' ENROLMENT CARD.

Name ...Raymond Maidstone...

Troop ...Barnwood Parish Church (11th Gloucester.)

Date of Enrolment ...22nd Nov. 1936...

Scoutmaster's Signature

E.H.J. Loott Vicar

P.J. Chapman.

The Enrolment Card of Raymond "Teddy" Maidstone who was one of the group of twelve scouts to be enrolled when the reformed troop began in 1936. He lived at Industry Cottages, opposite what is now the Deaf Community Centre, and attended Barnwood School and The Crypt. He became Barnwood's first King's Scout in November 1938 and was invited to take part in the St George's Day Parade at Windsor in 1939.

Just under five years later, on New Year's Day, 1944, he was killed whilst flying a Lancaster Bomber. He is pictured here in his RAF uniform, and is remembered on the Parish War Memorial.

When peace was eventually restored, both scouts and cubs began to meet regularly again with the first gatherings being held in October 1945 under Mr Wilkins. John Laughton, who had served in the Royal Navy during the war, followed Canon Noott as vicar and made a real effort to encourage scouting. For a while he acted as leader and hosted meetings in the vicarage (Barnwood Court) but, as numbers grew, they moved back to the Reading Room. Subscriptions, at this time, were one penny a week. A new scoutmaster, John Carter, then moved into the area and established the Troop as a thriving concern.

The first camp after the war was at Cranham; John Carter was unable to attend and so Brian Lewis took charge. Brian (who was later to become a Parish Councillor) was Troop Leader at the time and recalls that it was cold in the old wartime tents with no sleeping bags and only two folded blankets. As the country was still subject to rationing, food was in limited supply. Fortunately, the father of one scout was a grocer and so some extra provisions were available! Nevertheless, some gooey porridge and a thick slice of bread and margarine was the standard breakfast menu. Recalling a camp in 1950, when the only source of water was a stream and the area was inundated with adders, Brian reminisced that by then things were improving as equipment slowly became available.

At about this time two new recruits, Terry Newland and Anthony Howarth, joined the scouts. Terry's father was a baker and was therefore a ready source of bread rolls for hot dog stalls, and cakes for camps! No one realised then, but for over sixty years, Terry was to play a leading part in the success of the scout group. His involvement was, and still is, much admired and appreciated by the local scouting community. Anthony, too, was later to become a cub leader and, indeed, a District Commissioner.

The Reading Room, 1952. A quiz on the Highway Code being conducted by Idris David (centre front); he was both a Parish Councillor and a School Manager. Anthony Howarth is pictured on the extreme left, Terry Newland on the extreme right and Brian Lewis can be seen in the centre at the back.

In 1954, after the involvement of several other scout leaders, including Sidney "Bha" Shaw and Robert Herd (who always wore a kukri in his belt), Brian took charge of both cubs and scouts. Two years later Terry took over from Brian as leader of the scouts and then, after completing deferred National Service, Brian became a District Scoutmaster.

Throughout this time both the cubs and the scouts continued to meet at the Reading Room. The logistics of occupying forty young people in that small space necessitated plenty of planning as the cubs could prove to be quite a handful. In the warmer months many meetings were held outside with wide games being played regularly on Church Field, in Barnwood Copse or in the area around the gravel pits behind the old fire station (what is today Hammond Way and Barnett Way). On wet nights and in the winter, however, they had to make do with the Reading Room. Brian added to his popularity by telling scary stories which always ended at the exciting bit and were "to be continued next week".

But the Reading Room was too small; it had served its purpose and now a new, larger building was sought. Funds were raised, the Parish Council arranged for land to be leased and, eventually, a wooden scout hut was opened behind Wotton Hall Club on what is now the site of the school. This was to be the headquarters until, in 1976 and by this time no longer church sponsored, the group moved to a more substantial building in Hucclecote. Thus, after approaching half a century, the Barnwood Scouts became known as 11th Gloucester (Hucclecote) Scouts.

Top Left: "Ball in the Bucket" at Barnwood Court Fête in 1952.

Top Right: Cubs and helpers, 1951.

Bottom: Barnwood Scouts, early 1950s, with their aerial runway.

Flooding in Barnwood

Barnwood House Hospital used a sluice gate to control the amount of water released from its "lake". A heavy storm, circa 1964, was one of several occasions when the system failed and Church Lane became flooded.

The boundary wall of the Hospital, part of which is visible in the picture below, originally ran for several hundred metres along Church Lane. Many local residents believed that the broken glass on top of the wall was in place to keep patients inside the grounds but, this was not the case: the authorities considered it to be good protection from trespassers.

In July 2007, Gloucestershire suffered its most severe floods on record. The Mythe Water Treatment Works were affected and, consequently, much of Gloucester was left without running water. The sight of bowsers, (these were placed on the junction of Lilliesfield Avenue and North Upton Lane) will be a memory of many who lived in Barnwood at the time.

The Church Choir

Like so many rural churches of its age, Barnwood originally had a west gallery choir. During the 18th and 19th centuries, the singers and musicians sat in a gallery above the present vestry, in the space which is nowadays occupied by the organ pipes. Because they were not allowed to sing hymns (being the words of men) until 1820, originally they sang anthems, chants and psalms (all with words from the Bible). For many years the singers were accompanied by a barrel organ (which once went wrong and had to be wheeled into Church Field before it would stop playing!).

The Victorians generally disapproved of these Georgian galleries, and so they were taken down whenever feasible. Thus, the Barnwood gallery was removed during the 1874 restoration of the church and the choir then went into the chancel. By this time they were singing to the accompaniment of a hand pumped organ which had been donated by Colonel Dowling of Barnwood Court. The organ, sited in the chancel, was used until 1911, when it was replaced by an instrument provided by the Bonnor family. This, too, was hand pumped until well into the 1950s. (It became a tradition that two boys from the choir were given time off from Barnwood School in order to pump the organ for funerals; this was considered to be a very lucrative perk!)

Choir trips, which in time became almost an annual affair, had begun in September 1892 with a trip to Weston. The sands, paddling and donkey rides proved to be very popular. The 1894 visit to the same venue included a trip on the "Waverley" steamer.

Although women may well have been heard singing in the gallery, after the move to the east end of the church the choir was entirely male. This changed in March 1917 as a result of the war when, according to the parish magazine of the time, "the sadly depleted choir was supplemented by the assistance of four women and three elder girls from the Sunday afternoon choir".

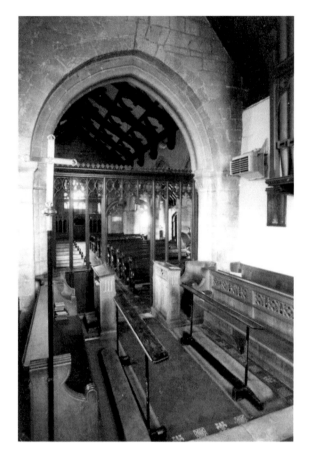

The choir and the organ were both situated in the chancel from 1874 until 1959. Two of the organ pipes can be seen in the top right of the picture; the console was positioned immediately below the pipes.

Throughout the years the attractions of Weston continued to have an appeal. Even though other venues were visited, including the Isle of Wight on one occasion, by 1930 the favoured venue was once again the Somerset coastline. In that year the choir returned to Gloucester after the trams had finished running and seven motor cars were dispatched from the parish to meet the train: Barnwood was clearly becoming affluent. Indeed, for a while, in the middle years of the century, the choir boys received a small payment for their services; there was even occasional talk of strikes when increases were not forthcoming!

The choir at Easter, 1931. On the extreme left is the organist and choirmaster, Mr R Leach, whilst the vicar, Canon Brice, may be seen on the right.

By 1959 the choir was again on the move. The choir stalls in the chancel were replaced and the choir relocated to the nave. In 1966 the present organ was installed at a cost of approximately £2500. Incorporating much pipework from the 1911 organ, the pipes were re-sited on a platform behind the screen at the west end of the church, in the position once occupied by the gallery choir. A detached organ console was placed behind the pulpit adjacent to the new choir stalls.

At about this time, too, the choir became truly mixed and has remained so until the present day, although the number of male trebles has declined greatly. Over the years the colour of the choir robes has changed twice. In about 1960 the traditional black gave way to red and then, in about 1990, the colour changed to blue. For a number of years now, the choir has been affiliated to the Royal School of Church Music.

The organist and choirmaster, George Williams, can be seen second from the right at the back in this 1952 photograph.

Outside the south door in 1961. The vicar, Michael Seacome, and the organist, George Williams, are in the centre of the picture.

The choir in 1984. Gordon John, the choirmaster and organist, appears on the left at the back. Asa Gee who was, for many years, the lay reader is standing on the extreme right.

The choir 2004; choir leader Vicki Barnes-Moffat is third from the right.

The "old" Barnwood Avenue

Originally, the Avenue was a private driveway serving as the entrance to Barnwood Court which was, for centuries, the only building in the Avenue. For many years this driveway was pillared and gated and only those who sought business at the Court were allowed to enter; but times changed. By the middle of the 19th century the public was enjoying access to this splendid tree-lined pathway. Families strolled, mothers pushed prams and visitors from around the area came to enjoy it.

The Avenue, circa 1900.

In 1865, one writer commented that "the noble avenue is an ornament to the neighbourhood. At summer sunset when the tapering trunks glow like burnished shafts, and the foliage hangs in dark green masses chequered with ruddy tints, and the long shadows stream across the gravel path below, the avenue seems like a spot enchanted".

Around 1889 a novel, essentially a Christmas story partly set in Barnwood, was published in Sheffield. The novelist wrote:

"...from what may be called the centre of Barnwood there branches an avenue of trees that is without its peer in picturesque effect for miles around. A procession of lime, ash, beech and chestnut trees makes a portal, as it were, to a grand Gothic aisle of green, formed by ancestral elms which have been a rook colony for this half-century or more. In the middle of this leafy colonnade the branches bend low to listen to the prattle of a baby brook which, by-and- by, throws its little cares under the protection of the Severn, flowing in majesty and strength in the great breadths of gentle green beyond.

Over this lisping streamlet spans a wooden-railed arch whereon beneath the luminous leaves, many a rustic Romeo has rehearsed the language of love with a west-country Juliet.

Beyond the avenue stands the church, square, short, squat, ugly with a square, short, squat, ugly tower."

The novel was not widely acclaimed – and particularly not in Barnwood!

At the end of the 19th century a pair of semi-detached dwellings, known as Eastgrove and Westgrove, became only the second building in the Avenue but little else was built until the years approaching the Second World War.

By this time, the trees were being felled to make way for the new development and a local writer was moved to pen the following piece which was published in both the parish magazine and *The Citizen*.

Long years ago an avenue of trees
Was planted by an owner of the Court:
The pride and joy of Barnwood and of those
From far and wide who came to visit here:
And many a generation, as they made their way,
Neath spreading boughs, to worship at their Church,
Thanked God for all the beauty of His Earth.
But now the trees are felled; felled ere their prime,
And Barnwood Avenue is dead.
The name alone remains

The Avenue, 1926

And generations, yet unborn, may ask
Why that plain road is called an avenue.
That must not be; the Avenue can't die
And in the place of trees long loved so well
New trees must grow.
For out of death springs life, and there must rise
An avenue more beautiful than we have known
To lead men to their Church
And to their God.

By Christmas 1939, the various changes had made the surface of the Avenue deteriorate to such an extent that there was concern that local people would be unable to walk to church for services. The vicar, Canon Noott, wrote that it was in a "terribly dilapidated state". He remarked that it was felt that the parishioners, having recently subscribed to purchase Church Field in order to preserve some open space and the view of the church, were now resigned to seeing the old Avenue disappear.

And disappear it did; "*the name alone remains*".

The Church in the Early 20th Century

Towards the end of the 19th century and during the first part of the 20th century the parish magazines were printed by F J Brooke, a printer and photographer who was based in Westgate Street. The vicar, Francis Harvie Fowler, had a very good relationship with Mr Brooke and occasionally used one of Mr Brooke's photographs in the magazine. Mr Brooke took a number of photographs of Barnwood, including this one which shows the church from the south west. Although there were many pictures of scenes, people and events taken in those years, sadly almost all have been lost.

The Parish Centre

By the 1980s, with the development first of Abbeydale and then of Abbeymead, Barnwood had become the fastest growing parish in Gloucestershire. The resulting changes meant that there were more young families in the parish and this presented the Parochial Church Council with a number of issues that needed to be addressed.

Although both St Oswald's in Coney Hill, and the newly built Christchurch in Abbeydale, had facilities suitable for the needs of a growing parish, St Lawrence's, the third member of the local ecumenical team, did not. Neither were there any plans in the new housing development for any community facilities close to St Lawrence's. Therefore, there was an urgent need for a centre for the church to use for its outreach to this rapidly growing community.

The newly built church school offered a large space for meetings, but this was only available out of school hours and the Reading Room was only suitable for small gatherings. More importantly, both buildings were some distance from the church and neither was suitable for a parish administrative centre.

Ever since Barnwood Court became a vicarage in the 1930s, its large rooms and facilities had been used by the parish for meetings and for social events. (Many still remember that, for a number of years, the youth club met in the cellar!) But, when the vicarage moved to the adjacent purpose-built bungalow, space was far more restricted. Yet still, on Sundays, the junior members of the church would meet in its lounge and garage before crossing the churchyard to join the adults at the morning service. After this service the vicarage was used for serving refreshments to the congregation. These arrangements were not ideal for an expanding church community.

Around 1990, therefore, the incumbent Peter Minall and the PCC started to look at the options available to resolve this shortcoming. Interestingly, the parish had faced a similar problem in the 1880s. Then, a suitable Institute or Parish Room, was sought both to house the community's library and as a building for social use by the people of Barnwood. The end result was the Barnwood Reading Room - although lack of finances meant that the final building was only a quarter of the size of the original design. Just over one hundred years later, therefore, the people of Barnwood were starting the process all over again. This time, however, the church initiated the process.

In 1991, with the retirement of Peter Minall and the appointment of Martin Riley, the project moved into its next phase. From the outset the church's planning authority, the Diocesan Advisory Committee, was involved. Because the church is a Grade 2* listed building English Heritage was also consulted. In 1992 five options were presented for consideration. A new building to the south of the church was the most popular option, although support was not unanimous; indeed some did not see that the project was necessary at all.

Early in 1993, a design brief was produced: a single storey was envisaged. Subsequently, the Diocesan Advisory Committee was asked for advice. It was supportive of the plans to build south of the church but was keen to see the proposed building brought into a positive relationship with the church building. Architects were approached and, by October 1994, the PCC was able to put to the Diocesan Advisory Committee some ideas from Francis Preston Roberts who was an award-winning architect from the North of England. He was much influenced by the Arts and Crafts Movement and had been specifically recommended for this job.

Initial estimates of the cost of the project were around £320K, but when planning consent was obtained in March 1996, these estimates had risen to £380K and the parish had to commit to raising this amount of money.

The main fundraising activity was a 'four year pledge' whereby individuals pledged to give a certain amount by the anticipated end of the project. This scheme allowed the fundraising committee to approach grant awarding bodies with evidence of a commitment by the parish. Other activities included a sponsored cycle ride, a "Music and Mince Pies Evening", "gourmet meals", an auction, an auction of promises and a sale of paintings. Also, an appeal was made to every other church in the country dedicated to St Lawrence. Businesses and individuals from the wider community were very supportive and the fund soon stood at over £110K. This amount was bolstered considerably when the Diocesan Properties Fund granted £180K towards the venture.

The Reverend R Coates cutting the first turf.

By the end of 1999, the building project was well under way, contractors had been appointed and signs of preparatory groundwork were evident. An earlier archaeological survey had confirmed that the proposed site was a mediaeval graveyard. In order to minimise the impact on this ancient site, the plans called for the building to be mounted on horizontal beams supported on deep, but narrow, piles rather than normal foundations. An archaeological dig had identified where there were remains which would be affected by the piles. Once all formal notifications had been given, these remains were exhumed and then re-interred close by.

One issue which resolved itself fairly easily was the matter of car parking. Planning consent had specified that twenty parking spaces should be provided. The old bus lay-by and turning area near the lych-gate site was no longer needed and so, after protracted discussions with the relevant authorities, this was converted into a car park.

After ten years the project was nearing completion. Martin Riley had moved on to a new incumbency and his successor, Robert Coates, saw the project through to its conclusion. The opening ceremony was held on Sunday 3rd June 2001, when the Bishop of Gloucester cut the tape.

The Bishop being diligently observed whilst cutting the tape.

Highways and Byways

Barnwood's earliest road dates back to the Roman occupation. It is the road that runs through the heart of the parish and is known as Barnwood Road. At various times it has also been called London Road, the Turnpike Road and Ermin Way. It follows part of the road which was originally built as a high speed route to enable Roman soldiers to move swiftly between the two centres of Cirencester and Gloucester. Whilst the old Roman road is Barnwood's spine there are several routes leading off it and away from the parish.

Upton Lane wound its way past agricultural land owned by Barnwood House Hospital, past a few isolated houses and the Coney Hill Hospital estate and eventually ended at Upton St Leonards. Local residents frequently used this tranquil road as a rural walk and as a source of succulent blackberries. The original road ran along what we now know as North Upton Lane, Upton Close and Abbeymead Avenue.

The old Upton Lane, looking towards Upton St Leonards, as the contractors move in. The entrance to Coney Hill Hospital's East Lodge is on the right; the Turmut-Hoer public house now stands on the left of this area.

The entrance to Upton Lane was flanked by two large houses. On the western side was Manor House, which was built around 1750 and still stands. This was once the home of Samuel and Ann Bubb who were grandparents of the scientist Sir Charles Wheatstone. It is believed that Wheatstone may have been born here and that he spent many of his school holidays here.

On the eastern side of the entrance stood Barnwood Lodge which, together with its extensive grounds, was replaced by housing in the late 1950s. Part of this development was named after the nearby Lilliesfield gravel pits; at one time a railed track ran from the gravel pits into Upton Lane. The Wotton Brook, which today borders Lilliesfield Avenue, was much wider in the days when it flowed through the grounds of Barnwood Lodge. Maps show clearly that the brook once split to form an island. Today only the southern branch of the brook remains.

Church Lane defined the westernmost extent of the estate of Barnwood House Hospital. After its sale, the development of the Hospital land to the west was known as Grovelands. This small estate probably takes its name from a house known as Grove Villa which originally stood in the grounds of Chalfont, just across the Lane. Church Lane, originally

The Lych-Gate, 1925

narrower than it is today, ran past Barnwood Copse (removed about 1960) and the church and eventually ended in Matson; in fact the route was sometimes referred to as "Matson Lane". The car park outside the parish centre served for some years as a bus terminus. Adjacent to this was the original site of the lych-gate which was the Parish War Memorial.

The Lodge, looking towards Church Lane.

On the other side of the road, opposite the church, the ground forms a 'balancing pond' for surface water from the adjoining housing estates. Once, there was a large house here called "The Lodge" (no connection with Barnwood Lodge mentioned earlier) which was used for various types of accommodation by Barnwood House Hospital. It was demolished around 1950. Beyond this were the Hospital's cricket pitch, cricket pavilion and chapel. Still there today, but now used as a weight training gymnasium, the chapel was built about 1875.

The third of the southbound routes leading away from the parish is Eastern Avenue. Built during the years just preceding the Second World War, and originally constructed with concrete sections, it was a tree-lined, almost rural road. Anti-aircraft guns were positioned along this route during the war and RAF Barnwood, which was at one time the RAF Record Office, was situated close to the site of the present Homebase store.

Local residents often took advantage of the excellent weather forecasts provided by this station!

The RAF Station in Eastern Avenue.

Today, Corinium Avenue leads away from Barnwood in a northerly direction. This is a modern route built in the latter half of the twentieth century over fields once owned by Barnwood House Hospital. The only other northern bound exit from the parish is not a road at all; it is Welveland Lane.

A map of 1780 shows that this lane led to an area referred to as "Wellfurlong", from which the name "Welveland" may well have been derived. The land to the west was known as Sand Field. Welveland Lane and the track beyond have long been recognised as a route from Barnwood to Churchdown. The Salutation Inn, which was demolished in 1817, is believed to have stood close to the entrance to Welveland Lane for 150 years. Barnwood House Hospital farm buildings, some of which can still be seen, were built on the eastern side of the lane. The properties on the western side were built by the Hospital to accommodate staff. Around 1970, after a campaign by a local civil engineer, Neil James, the track was developed into a path suitable for bicycles. It has been further widened in recent times.

This 1960s picture illustrates how, in the middle of the 20th century, Barnwood was changing from a rural parish. It shows cows being taken across the recently constructed bridge (close to what is now Sainsbury's) along the track into Welveland Lane; they are destined for milking at Barnwood House Farm. The chimney of the Hospital's boiler house can be seen in the distance across the fields.

The Retirement of the Coombers

After many years of loyal service to the school Mr & Mrs Coomber finally retired as caretakers in July 1980. They are pictured in the centre having just received a gift from the children. There are some other well known faces too. On the left are Mr & Mrs Etheridge who had run the shop opposite the school since about 1950. Mr Etheridge attended many school Christmas parties in his role as Father Christmas. Next to them are Mr & Mrs George Smith; Mrs Smith had been a Sunday School teacher with Mrs Coomber in the 1950s and Mr Smith is still remembered for his contribution to the life of the Reading Room. Mr John Thorne was the headteacher at the time of the presentation and he is standing next to Mrs Smith. On the far right of the picture are three former teachers, Mrs Warren, Mr Parry and Mrs Haines.

The Church Bell Renovation

Although five of the bells have been in the tower since 1698 (their history is covered in our earlier book, *Tales of Old Barnwood*) the ring was only augmented from six to eight when major works were executed in 1913. By coincidence, 100 years after they were last removed from the tower, the church bells were taken out again, in February 2013, in order to facilitate refurbishment and restoration.

The main reason for this was that several centuries of wear had caused some of the bells to weaken and become liable to crack. Adjustments had been made in 1913 whereby the bells were turned so that the clappers would strike them in a different place. But, after another 100 years of wear, new indentations were clearly visible. Therefore some of the bells were removed to undergo specialist welding in order to rebuild the worn areas. Other works included the replacement of the original, plain white metal bearings with ball bearings for every bell.

The removal of the six bells in 1913.

In order to remove the bells from the tower, a new trap door had to be constructed in the vestry ceiling. This was because the trap door used a century earlier was obstructed by the "new" organ pipes immediately beneath it.

The total cost of these remedial works was in the region of £35000. Several grants were made to cover the cost and there were generous donations both from individuals and businesses.

The tenor being taken out of the vestry in 2013. The gate had to be removed to allow the bell to pass through the doorway.

The bells lined up outside the south door, February 2013.

The treble bell, which was dedicated in 1913 to the churchwardens, one of whom was Walter B Wood.

Bell Inscriptions

The Barnwood bells are inscribed as follows:

Treble
: *"Now I am cast we're eight at last 1913*
Walter B Wood John M Buchanan Churchwardens"

Second
: *"Saint Lawrence 1913*
Ring in the love of truth and right Francis Harvie Fowler
Vicar"

Third
: *"Cast by John Warner & Sons London 1873*
In memoriam Mariae Uxoris Dilectae D. D. Jacobus
Henricus Dowling"

Fourth
: *"God save the King A R 1698"*

Fifth
: *"Peace and good neighbourhood Abbra: Ruddhall 1698"*

Sixth
: *"In 98 all we were cast we were but 4 at first now 6 at last"*

Seventh
: *"Wm: Blizard Sam: Collerick church wardens: A: R: 1698"*

Tenor
: *"God: Prosper: This: Parish: William: Johnson: Gent: A R 1698"*